CRUISING THROUGH THE STOCK MARKET
Winning Strategies for WORKING PROFESSIONALS

SHAILESH JHA

INDIA · SINGAPORE · MALAYSIA

Notion Press Media Pvt Ltd

No.50, Chettiyar Agaram Main Road,
Vanagaram, Chennai, Tamil Nadu – 600 095

First Published by Notion Press 2021
Copyright © Shailesh Jha 2021
All Rights Reserved.

ISBN 978-1-63806-756-6

This book has been published with all efforts taken to make the material error-free after the consent of the author. However, the author and the publisher do not assume and hereby disclaim any liability to any party for any loss, damage, or disruption caused by errors or omissions, whether such errors or omissions result from negligence, accident, or any other cause.

While every effort has been made to avoid any mistake or omission, this publication is being sold on the condition and understanding that neither the author nor the publishers or printers would be liable in any manner to any person by reason of any mistake or omission in this publication or for any action taken or omitted to be taken or advice rendered or accepted on the basis of this work. For any defect in printing or binding the publishers will be liable only to replace the defective copy by another copy of this work then available.

Contents

Foreword..5
Acknowledgement 7

Chapter 1   Additional Income and Stock Market 9

   1.1   Why I wrote this book..11
   1.2   My Journey with Stock Market..........................15
   1.3   Additional Source of Income 21
   1.4   Stock Market as Additional Source of Income.....25
   1.5   Working Professionals: Challenges in
        the Stock Market 29

Chapter 2   Things to Know Before Investing 37

   2.1   Commonly used Terms and Basic
        Information for Beginners 39
   2.2   Stock Market – Products.......................................65
   2.3   Products and Associated Risks 69
   2.4   Advantages of Investing in Stock Market 71
   2.5   Important Ratios and Things to Know
        Before Investing..77
   2.6   Sectors - Its Performance and Analysis 89
   2.7   Picking the Right Stock in the Stock Market 157
   2.8   Technical Analysis of Stock................................161
   2.9   The Power of Compounding 187
  2.10 Attitude for Success 191

Contents

Chapter 3 Planning and Execution for Investment 195

- 3.1 Goal Setting..197
- 3.2 Plan and Prepare to Invest in the Stock Market 203
- 3.3 Portfolio Building..225
- 3.4 Winning Strategies for Working Professionals...231
- 3.5 Common Mistakes of Investors 261
- 3.6 Risk Management..269

Chapter 4 Facts and Myth of Stock Market 283

- 4.1 Misconceptions of the Stock Market.................285
- 4.2 How much Return to expect from Stock Market 291
- 4.3 Performance of BSE Sensex over the years.........293
- 4.4 The Equity/Investment Advisor........................297

Summary 301

Foreword

Financial independence is goal that every individual desires to have early in their life. However this is something neither taught in the schools nor gets inherited from others. At most what we learn from our parents is to open a savings account and rely on decreasing interest rate from banks. For a middle class worker, salaried income is the main source of income. In day to day's struggle to raise a family and support their dependents, one hardly has time, knowledge and means to do more than opening savings deposits and mutual funds. These financial strategies does not provide any financial independence to the earners. Robert Allen, a motivational speaker and renowned investing advisor rightly says "How many millionaires do you know who have become wealthy by investing in savings accounts". Therefore stock market becomes a good viable option not only to plan your constant income but also for financial security and independence for future. The challenge with stock market is that you are literally looking for a needle in the haystack. There are too many variables to account for and there are too many choices to make from. Again no one teaches us about how to invest in the stock market and make money. There are numerous books and perhaps YouTube videos on investing but most of them either talk theory or are made for astute investors. There is a need for a book which can talk to me in a conversational language, which can explain me the concepts and strategies with someone's practical experience. This is exactly what Shailesh has done in this book.

Shailesh has imprinted his wealth of knowledge collected over 25 years during many ups and downs of the market, in this book. He explains not only the fundamentals like power of compounding but also practical strategies for being successful in achieving your financial goals. The author makes the case for starting early from his personal experience and then he goes on to describe strategies for both short term income generation to aid your monthly cash flow as well as long term investing strategies to fulfill your desire for financial independence. I found this book literally talking to me face to face with its simplicity yet dives deeper into deriving my own plans for success.

Happy reading and happy planning for your future!

– Sujit Kumar
Founder and President at Agora,
Houston, TX

Acknowledgement

Writing this book is like dream coming true to me. The Stock Market has been a passion for me since the day I got my first salary. During the initial years, it was a real challenge to generate consistent income from the stock market. I struggled for many years to learn the stock market intricacies to invest profitably alongside my regular job.

I persisted despite my initial setbacks and eventually formed an investing strategy which brought forth good results. My Risk Management Strategy can be followed by all working professionals who would like to invest in the stock market.

I thank my Wife for her whole-hearted support during my Journey of investing, learning and then writing this book.

I thank my parents and all family members for encouraging me to write this book.

My special thanks to Kislaya who helped me in designing all the images of the book and Prachi Jha, Sneha Smriti and Bhuwaneshwaree for their contributions and help in completion of the book.

I also thank the 1995 batch of IIT(ISM), Dhanbad, for their support and encouragement in writing the book as well as for being my motivation.

Acknowledgement

I would like to thank all those who encouraged me to pen down my thoughts in this book.

Last but not the least, thanks to the publishing team for their efforts to publish the book.

Chapter 1

Additional Income and Stock Market

1.1 Why I wrote this book

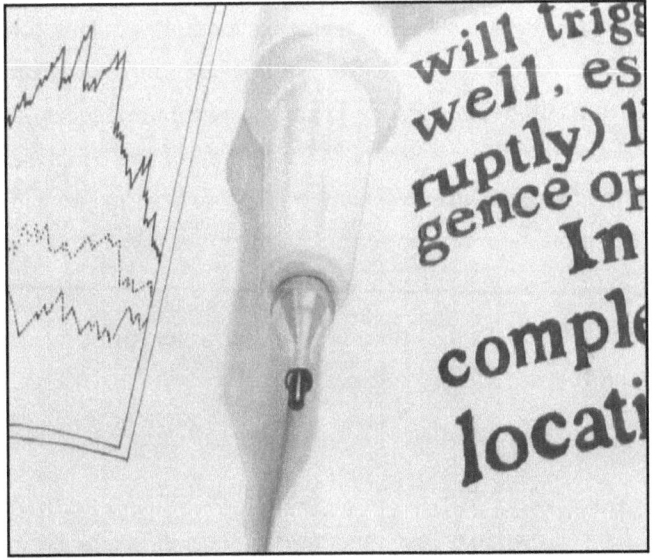

The need to write this book has risen after understanding the aspirations, desires, and interests of almost all the working professionals across industries. Being from the same fraternity, the challenges and the day to day issues propping up are well known to me. The growing private sector has created a lot of jobs, but what is evident is the prevailing uncertainty. The

"Never depend on single Income. Make investments to create a second source." – Warren Buffett

percentage of the yearly increment has come down drastically these days. The IT industry has set an example and mobilized a practice of declining increments which many sectors have started following.

Companies are opting for all cost-cutting measures possible, including giving pink slips to professionals. This has led to the advancement of a situation where most employees look for a fallback strategy to generate an extra/passive source of income that can compensate for the inflation and minimal increment provided by the employers. While most of the employees want additional income, many want to switch over to some other profession and opportunity which can give greater job satisfaction as well as better income.

Some of the things that are common for most of the employees are:

- Job insecurity
- Following the same day to day routine
- Low salary increment level in most of the industries
- Struggle for promotion
- Cartel and Politics at work place
- Unreasonable bosses
- The job and assignment given is not as per the talent and skill
- Underutilization of talent and skillset

"Every day is a bank account, and time is our currency. No One is rich, no one is poor, we have got 24 hours each. – Christopher Rice

- Limited growth due to skillset, location, size of the company, and other factors
- Far from home/native place
- Difficulty in getting leave during urgency and genuine exigencies
- Daily long travel to work place
- Chances of frequent change in job location and transfer to an unwanted location
- Fear of sector, industry, or company not performing well
- Low or no disbursement of the variable component of salary
- Minimum scope for change or upgrade of skillset

The above factors make every employee look for an option that can

- Provide additional income generation
- Provide a reliable fallback strategy and plan B
- Provide some change and excitement in day to day activities and chores
- Enhance knowledge in an area other than the ongoing job/work
- Can be done in parallel to the existing/ongoing job

"One of the very nice things about investing in the stock market is that you learn about all different aspects of the economy. It's your window into a very large world." – Ron Chernow

- Has an easy entry to start with
- Can have an easy exit if needed
- Needs minimum investment to start
- **Helps create wealth in long run**

The Stock Market provides an excellent option to all the employees to explore and amass wealth slowly and consistently. **But it demands proper management of the risk involved.** If a systematic and disciplined investment is done regularly and consistently, the risk can be managed leading to wealth creation in the long run.

"There's no such thing as a value company. Price is all that matters. At some price, an asset is a buy, at another it's a hold, and at another it's a sell." – Seth Klarman

1.2 My Journey with Stock Market

The stock Market captivates many and I was no exception to this. The era when Doordarshan used to telecast news in English and Hindi, twice, having an update on the Stock Market Indices, is still fresh in my mind.

Update on Stock Market and Sensex used to create curiosity about it and I wanted to delve more into it. There was no one in proximity who could elaborate on the nuances of this arcane stock market to me.

"There are no secrets to success. It is the result of preparation, hard work, and learning from failure." – Colin Powell

My journey with the stock market started some 25 years ago, when I started earning from my debut job with Gujarat Ambuja Cements in Gujarat after passing out from IIT (ISM), Dhanbad. Since I wanted to understand the stock market deeper, I ordered a book on Stock Market. It gave me preliminary insight into the stock market on how different companies have performed in the past and what kind of profit they have provided to the stockholders. This book answered most of the questions I had in mind before getting ready to start as a small investor in the stock market.

Once phase 1 of knowing the basics of the stock market ended, my 2nd phase commenced, where I started making some small investments to test my luck. I purchased some stocks of Reliance Industries and a few more blue chip ones. In those days, electronic form of buying and selling of shares was not available, hence I had to venture some twenty kilometers from my work site to a stockbroker to manage transactions. This continued for some time and later I had to move out of Gujarat into the next company of Vedanta Resources and at this point in time, I decided to sell my shares and move on. I could only book profit on a few and had to incur losses on the remaining few. Since my investment was low, it didn't pinch me.

I reentered the stock market again when Demat accounts started getting opened for investors and transactions went electronic. Share transaction became significantly easier and most of the risks associated with paper certificates were alienated.

"Wealth is when small efforts produce big results. Poverty is when big efforts produce small results." – Unknown

Also, the availability of internet at almost all locations augmented reach of stock markets to various demographics and gave fair independence on transactions based on individual research. Buoyed by the wave, I too started my research on the stock market and planned to evolve on investment strategy.

Having no precursory knowledge and guidance on the stock market, I made a strategy of investing in companies with strong fundamentals. I shortlisted companies which had good market capitalization, good sales, good profit, and consistent growth for last three years. I was ignorant of the different ratios which let us know about the different factors of the companies which facilitate investment decisions.

I started getting good result on my investment, based on my very raw method of selecting the stocks, i.e. based on just a few factors, like Market Capitalization, Sales, Profit, Product market share, and reputation/goodwill of the companies for investment. This gave me confidence and motivated me to invest and give more time and effort into the stock market. Being a full-time employee, it was always a challenge to keep track of various companies and monitor the stocks and their performances, so my investments automatically became long term investments. So, I used to buy the stock after doing basic fundamental analysis based on my home grown criteria and used to park it for some time. I found, that in short term most of the stocks were giving losses whereas when I kept them invested for some time, most of them used to give good returns.

"Tell me and I forget. Teach me and I remember. Involve me and I learn." – Benjamin Franklin

This suited me as I could focus on my job without bothering much about the stock market and also, my investment started getting enough time to mature and yield good returns.

Later, I started exploring more about fundamental analysis and technical analysis on the internet. It was then that I realized that there is a plethora of things to understand and become an astute investor. I was unaware of technical analysis for a considerable time and hence did not know when to buy, when to sell and when to average out the cost of the stock. This led me to incur heavy losses in a few of the stocks as I was chasing some of them when they started falling. Also, some of the stocks turned out to be real disasters for me as gradually they sank. My hopes that someday there would be sunshine on those stocks went in vain. Also, some of the investments never grew as these were stable stocks and had no movement over a longer period of time. There were many more leanings in the initial phase of my life as an investor. I was inquisitive of finding a panacea for cutting losses and always be prolific on my investments.

Also, as a full time working professional, I was facing challenges like:

Inability to do enough research on the Fundamentals of the companies

Inability to do any Technical analysis for deciding on buying and selling

> *"An investment in knowledge always pays the best interest. Learning is to the Studious, and Riches to the Careful. If a man empties his purse into his head, no man can take it away from him." – Jack Bogle*

Inability to take advantage of some of the stocks yielding very good returns which used to become every investor's delight

Inability to come out of stocks in time, and hence face the wrath of relentless losses with the plummeting of these stocks

Inability to handle my investments when there was a market crash or a sudden, big fall in the indices

This made many investments go wrong and obviously, I needed to find a solid solution.

I decided to learn Technical analysis, which I was absolutely unaware of, and wanted to get deeper knowledge on fundamentals and different ratios which could help me cut my losses and start giving me good results on my investment. I attended a few classes to understand these topics and got a deeper insight into the Fundamental and Technical analysis together, which led me to come up with my final strategy on Risk Management.

In this period not only did I gain knowledge on Intraday trading, futures, and Options, but also tried investing to understand these products and check for their feasibility for investment for working professionals.

I finally derived a strategy which was based more on hedging and Risk Management Strategy, which gave me

"Investing in yourself is the best thing you can do, and as a part of investing in yourself, you should learn more about money management." – Warren Buffett

regular return from the market. With my continuous efforts to explore new things and strategies which could work for working professionals who have less time to devote to the Stock market and yet have propensity for investing, I derived a Strategy for Working Professionals.

This Risk Management Strategy helps working professionals to invest with

> **Peace of mind in the stock market**
>
> **Overall good profit on the portfolio made**
>
> **Get Regular Returns from the Stock Market**
>
> **Take care of Market Volatility**
>
> **Manage your investment and make them profitable even when the market crashes**

This encouraged me to share my thought process with all so that investing in stock market, turns out to be profitable to most of the working professionals, without having to explore for years to devise a strategy and method for making profit from stock market which I had to go through.

The detailed learnings and strategies are described in this book.

"When you work on something that only has the capacity to make you 5 dollars, it does not matter how much harder you work – the most you will make is 5 dollars." – Idowu Koyenikan

1.3 Additional Source of Income

Most of the working professionals need to create at least one additional/extra/passive source of income to mitigate the risk of generating less income through active source of income and to reduce the risk of facing a survival problem in case of an unfortunate loss of the sole active source of income. People need to learn to earn more than the previous year to cope up with increasing inflation and the desire for a better lifestyle along with the wealth creation. The additional source of income can turn out to be a major corpus fund at the time of retirement if it is reinvested and has kept growing from the time the investment begins.

"You can only be financially free when your passive income exceeds your expenses." – T. Harv Eker

Moreover, a single source of income is risky as it puts tremendous pressure on the work front, resulting in cascading effects on family and health. As a consequence, the stress level of most working professionals is on the rise.

An economic crisis or a pandemic like situation is usually unpredictable and loss of job in such a scenario brings enormous pressure on survival.

Moreover, at the time of crisis, taking the risk to invest whatever is left to start a new set up for income generation may turn out to be devastating.

Most of us have an active source of income (Job, business, etc.) as the main source of income, and we need a few additional passive sources of income, which can be used for

- Taking care of family and self in case of loss of an active source of income
- Taking care of additional fund required during exigency
- Taking care of fund required at the time of retirement
- Providing some options to learn and develop an additional skillset
- Paying off debts
- Savings for big expenses
- Helping us to reach our financial goal sooner
- Figuring out new business idea and their execution

"The key to financial freedom and great wealth is a person's ability or skill to convert earned income into passive income and/or portfolio income." – Robert Kiyosaki

There are different ways of making the additional passive source of income, like creating YouTube videos, making a mobile app, selling of products online or through direct selling concept, freelancing, writing and publishing books, investing in real estate and investing in the stock market. Every passive money-making avenue has its advantages and disadvantages, but based on the interest, time available and skill set, the right kind of passive income source can be selected and worked upon to generate an additional source of income.

While most of the passive sources of income generation take time to establish before giving result, there are few which start generating the revenue from the day one starts working on it. For instance, providing tuition, working as visiting faculty, online part-time job, freelancing, etc.

"As the economy is shifting, you need to have legitimate and creative source of extra income. There are opportunities available that people have been using for years now." – Franklin Gillette

1.4 Stock Market as Additional Source of Income

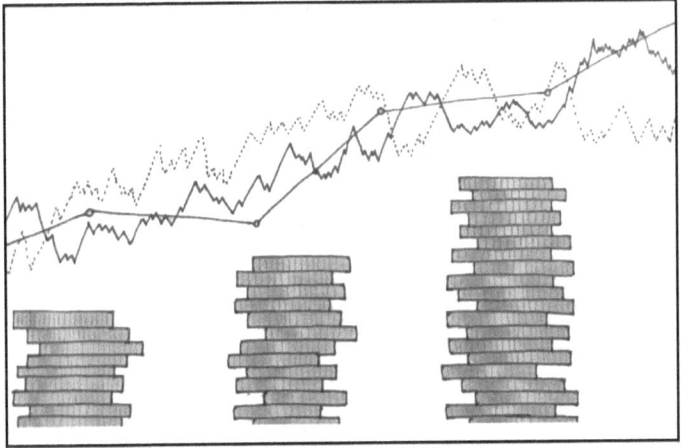

The Stock Market provides an additional source of Income to all those who are ready to invest in it in a systematic, regular, and disciplined way.

The actual wealth creators in any society are the businessmen. So, we can take advantage of a business that has already been set up, by investing in the Stock capital established by successful businessmen through stock markets.

"The Longer you are not taking action, the more money you are losing." – Carrie Wilkerson

Stock Market provides

- An easy entry
- An easy exit, if needed
- Option to start with small amount for investment
- Time to learn slowly and gear up for big income
- Inputs and guidance to invest from experts
- Learn and research at our end as most of the data are available online
- Make big and sumptuous amount in the long run

Most of the people, who have invested in the right stocks that remained invested for a considerably longer period, have made good returns on their investment.

The stock market serves as a good source of additional income and can become a primary source of income once the rules and tricks of the game are understood.

Investment in the stock market demands time and effort to research so that investment is made in only those companies which are going to give good returns on investment. Hence an investment in the stock market calls for greater responsibility, discipline, and knowledge to be successful.

Speculative investment in the stock market inevitably leads to loss and erosion of capital invested.

"You cannot have a million-dollar dream with a minimum wage work ethic." – Stephan C. Hogan

Investing and earning through the stock market has several associated advantages too and some of them are listed below:

- It can be done based on the availability of time and money.
- There is neither a need for expenses on any additional infrastructure, nor a need for any direct or indirect cost.
- No effect of local hindrances, lockdown, closure, weather, and similar challenges.
- No location constraint.
- It can be done online from anywhere.
- No need to take leave, nor fear any action for not being on the job in the stock market. Rather, it is suggested to take a few days of break time to time from the market for better returns. So, not being on the job (inactivity) for some time is an advantage in the stock market.
- No need to keep separate details of the transactions done. All details are available online and can be accessed any time.
- In general, if we invest in the right stock, the more time we remain invested, the better returns can be expected. So once invested, no action is required for a long period of time.

"Money is not the most important thing in the world. Love is. Fortunately I Love Money." – Jackie Mason

- Gain knowledge about the stock market, high performing companies, poor performing companies, growing companies, world stock market, economy, and many other related topics and events across the world.

- A possibility to work on off days and make a strategy for investment

- The possibility to buy and sell Equities on off days/ holidays, off working hours which gets automatically executed on the next working day.

- Set the target for the buying or sale of a Stock and forget it, which gets executed automatically once the target is achieved.

- The plethora of winning strategy is available which we need to explore and ascertain if it works for us.

"Money is always eager and ready to work for anyone who is ready to employ it." – Idowu Koyenikan

1.5 Working Professionals: Challenges in the Stock Market

Most of the working professionals want to invest in the stock market, but they struggle on many fronts when it comes to investing in the stock market and most of the them narrow down to one single point and that is the **unavailability of time to explore the stock market.**

As most of the working professionals' work is scheduled for 8 to 9 hours with additional time involved for commutation,

"My favorite things in life don't cost any money. It's really clear that the most precious resource we all have is time." – Steve Jobs

it is very difficult to find time for investing and monitoring in the stock market.

This results in making some hurried decisions. Input received like a suggestion from a friend, tips from the stock market brokers and others become the base and source of information for deciding the investment and picking the stock from the stock market.

The outcome of such investment is a loss on the investment made as it lacks planning and strategy for investment.

Following add up to the misery for working professionals:

Incredible Volume and Speed of Information from the Stock Market and Brokers

Today the challenge for working professionals is to manage the sheer speed and volume of information that keeps on coming from TV, Social Media, Brokers, and other similar sources. This confuses the working professionals more and it becomes difficult to filter out the right information. When there are so much informations available at any given time, it is always difficult to identify what is right and important and what needs to be picked up for investment.

Sometimes the information and analysis may be correct but we may not understand it. Like information may be for short term investment whereas we go for long term investment and such investment will eventually make a loss.

"The easiest way to manage your money is to take it one step at a time and not worry about being perfect." – Ramit Sethi

Not Enough Time to do Research and Analysis

Since we invest our hard earned money, it is always necessary to do essential research and analysis before investing it, but this is the most challenging part for working professionals as they generally do not get enough time after office hours to devote to the stock market for research and analysis.

Reactionary Market

Even if we have a source of the right kind of information we may get into trouble as the market sentiment and reactions are extreme many a times based on some bad or good news or policies that may come up from the company, Government, or any other source which may completely swing the direction of the stock.

Market reactions may get extreme, and the increasing global reach to the information has given investors more reasons to overreact.

For working professionals, it is almost impossible to track such information and react quickly to buy or sell the stock to save the investment or make a profit.

Such events lead to a major change in the way any stock behaves and it becomes very difficult to manage the stock for its good return unless and until **we have the right backup strategy planned to mitigate such risks that prop up in the market.**

"If you are not successful, that means you're not making enough mistakes." – Robert Kiyosaki

Insider Trading

Insider trading is another risk that can impact the investment of working professionals as they cannot get any clue about such trading that may happen.

Insider trading is buying or selling shares of a publicly-traded company by someone who has non-public, price-sensitive, and material information about that stock. An individual who has access to insider information would have an unfair edge over other investors, who do not have the same information and could potentially make large profits at the cost of other investors. Insider trading includes tipping others when we have any sort of non-public information.

Insiders could be like promoters, directors, auditors, and senior executives of the company etc. who have access to the company's information before it is disseminated to stock exchanges.

Insider trading is another risk that anyone can have when someone invests in the stock market. This risk exists for everyone including working professionals.

The Countless Choices of Stocks

There are more than 5000 companies listed on BSE and more than 1600 listed on NSE. This includes all kinds of stocks and shortlisting a few out of these becomes a horrendous

> *"With a good perspective on history, we can have a better understanding of the past and present, and thus a clear vision of the future."*
> *– Carlos Slim Helu*

task for everyone including working professionals. Analyzing all these stocks will need a lot of time and effort. With the availability of so many stocks and paucity of time, investors tend to take the easy route and hence the business of tips has started flourishing.

A plethora of choices in the Stock Market itself is enough to create confusion on where to invest.

Price Rigging in Stock Market

Price rigging is a form of market manipulation on price of stock. It is a conspiracy to keep prices as high as possible, it may also be employed to keep prices stable, fix them, or discount them.

In the Stock market manipulation is done by operators, promoters, or bull and bear cartels. Common investors who buy such shares find the prices of those shares adversely affected and may lose their money.

Working Professionals are more prone to such risks as they are not able to understand the background of such changes in the price and by the time it is noticed, people might already suffer major loss on their investment.

"Many people rush into the game of investing thinking they are predators. When they get to the middle of the game, they then realize they are the prey and try to escape but it will be too late. Only the preys with a well-defined exit strategy will escape, the rest will be slaughtered by the real predators." – Ajaero Tony Martins

Following the Crowd

Due to dearth of time, working professionals have herd mentality of following the crowd, which leads to losses.

The randomness of Foreign Institutional Investors (FIIs) and Domestic Institutional Investors (DIIs)

Fund inflow or outflow from Indian stock markets by FIIs/DIIs are quite unpredictable. As a result of such unpredictable and fast-paced moves by FIIs/DIIs, common investors are at the receiving end.

Those who remain alert to the market and monitor it on daily basis can take corrective actions against such randomness, whereas it becomes a difficult task for working professionals to react to the market's ups and down so quickly. Sometimes such movements are favorable and investors get good returns too.

Global Effect on Stock Market

Stock markets are integrated with the world market and any drastic up/down move in the markets of other major countries affects Indian stock markets too. Although the financials of Indian companies do not change with such moves in the world market, the prices of Indian stock are affected accordingly.

> *"I don't look to jump over seven-foot bars; I look around for one-foot bars that I can step over." — Warren Buffett*

Due to less time available to working professionals for the stock market, they are unable to monitor various global indices and developments. As a result, they are unable to take preemptive investment actions at appropriate time to react accordingly.

Companies Corporate Governance Issues

Small and mid-cap companies, sometimes may have poor Corporate Governance ethics and standards. Major stakeholders and Promoters in these companies may indulge in unethical business practices like fund diversion, fudging of accounts, and some other transactions which may not be as per company business and law, etc. Such dubious practices may start getting reflected in some way or the other on the chart of the company's stock after sometime. It may also be picked up by news agencies and may come in the media too. But by the time it reaches the common investors and working professionals, the share prices already get adjusted, leaving no option but to watch and feel defeated and lost.

No Access to Right Advices in Stock Market

It's risky to start investing without any guidance especially when one is a novice in investing in the stock market. It is estimated that around 90-95 percent of the investors lose money and the major reason is the learning curve of

"The stock market is filled with individuals who know the price of everything, but the value of nothing." – Phillip Fisher

individuals, which makes most of us lose money in the process of learning. If we come across someone who can help us to minimize the losses initially and guide us to make reasonable returns from the stock market, it will be a boon for the working professionals and others who enter new in the stock market to invest.

"In order to be successful, you have to make sure that being rejected doesn't bother you at all." – Bill Ackman

Chapter 2: Things to Know Before Investing

2.1 Commonly used Terms and Basic Information for Beginners

Since this book is written mainly for beginners in the stock market who have just started or are yet to start, it is important to know all the important basic terms being used in the stock market. Hence this chapter is included at the start of the book so that these frequently used terms can be understood easily while going through different chapters of the book.

"Stock market corrections, although painful at the time, is actually a very healthy part of the whole mechanism, because there are always speculative excesses that develop, particularly during the long bull market." – Ron Chernow

Share Market

It is a place where we can buy or sell shares. All stock exchanges across the world are part of the share market. Stock exchanges are secondary markets, where existing owners of shares can transact with potential buyers.

Face Value

When a company issues shares, each share has a face value. This refers to the value of the stock at the time of issuance. The company that issues the stock decides the face value and it does not change over time. Par value and face value mean the same thing.

Stock Exchange

This is a specific facility or a place in which different investments are traded.

Stock Share

Also known as common share, a Stock share represents a form of fractional ownership in a company. It is a vital source of raising capital.

"Of the billionaires I have known, money just brings out the basic traits in them. If they were jerks before they had money, they are simply jerks with a billion dollars." – Warren Buffett

In other words, if we own a sizeable amount of Stock Shares of a firm, we have the right to have our say in the company's affairs.

Stock Share Symbol

A Stock Share symbol is a code that represents a publicly-traded company on a stock exchange.

Bull Market

When stock prices in a market are generally rising, it is called a bull market. It's the opposite of a bear market. A single stock can be bullish or bearish too, and so can a sector or stock market as a whole.

Bear Market

The exact opposite of a bull market is a bear market – when the stock prices in the market are generally falling it is called a bear market. This is the opposite of a bull market. If a stock price plummets, it's bearish.

Quote

Price Information on a stock's latest trading price tells us its quote. This is sometimes delayed for a few min unless we're using an actual broker trading platform.

"It's better to hang out with people better than you. Pick out associates whose behavior is better than yours and you'll drift in that direction."
– Warren Buffett

Order

It is a show of intent to buy or sell shares in a given price range. For example, we may place an order to buy up to 100 shares of Company A, at a maximum price of Rs. 80 per share.

Bid

Our bid is the amount that we are willing to pay for a share. It's balanced against the asking price, which is what a seller wants per share of that same stock, and the spread is the difference between those two prices.

Ask

Ask is the price at which we are willing to sell a share.

Bid-ask Spread

This is the difference between the amount people are willing to spend to buy a share and the amount at which the shareholders are willing to sell a share. A trade can only happen when this spread is resolved. That is if the lowest price at which a share for Company A is being sold is 60, and the highest price someone is willing to pay for such a share is

"If you get to my age in life and nobody thinks well of you, I don't care how big your bank account is, your life is a disaster." – Warren Buffett

58 – no trade can happen. The trade can only happen when the bid and ask prices match.

Market Order

An order to sell/buy shares at the market price is called a market order. It is advisable to avoid placing a market order as the trade price can be very volatile.

Limit Order

An order to sell shares above a set price or buy shares below a set price is called a limit order. We should always use limit orders to trade shares.

Day Order

An order that is good only till the end of the trading day is called a "day order". If the order does not get executed by the time the market closes, it would be canceled.

Good-till-canceled Order

An order that will stay open until it is either executed or manually canceled. Such orders may stand for weeks if no shares are available to trade in the price range specified.

"I don't think there is any other quality so essential to success of any kind as the quality of perseverance. It overcomes almost everything, even nature." – John D. Rockefeller

Liquidity

Liquidity refers to how easily a stock can be sold off. A share that can be sold off quickly i.e. has high trade volumes is said to be highly liquid.

Trading Volume

The number of shares being traded is called trading volumes. The number of shares of stock traded during a particular time period, normally measured in average daily trading volume. Volume can also mean the number of shares we purchase of a given stock.

IPO/Initial Public Offering

In IPO, a company offers its share for the first time for trading on a stock exchange. Typically, in secondary market, we buy shares from the previous owner of the share and not the company directly. But in the case of an IPO, we get to buy the shares directly from the company.

Mutual Funds

Mutual funds are a way of investing across a large number of stocks by pooling our funds with other investors. This allows us to diversify our investment even if we have limited funds.

"Success is walking from failure to failure with no loss of enthusiasm."
– Winston Churchill

Further, a fund manager takes care of selecting the right stocks to invest in.

Exchange-Traded Funds

These are mutual funds that we can trade like shares on the stock exchange. They usually track an index. In other words, an exchange traded fund is a type of security that tracks an index, sector, commodity, or other asset, but which can be purchased or sold on a stock exchange in the same way as a regular stock.

Index

A stock market index is a statistical measure that reflects the changes in the stock market. It is created by picking and grouping similar kinds of stocks from the listed securities on the exchange.

Criteria for stock selection may depend on the type of industry, market capitalization, and size of the company. BSE Sensex and NSE Nifty are the two most widely used stock indices in India. This is also a benchmark that is used by investors and portfolio managers to measure market performance and performance of different stocks.

Market capitalization

It's the aggregate valuation of a firm based on the current share price multiplied by the total number of outstanding

"The best thing that happens to us is when a great company gets into temporary trouble...We want to buy them when they're on the operating table." – Warren Buffett

stocks. For example, if a company has 2 Cr outstanding shares with the current market price being Rs. 100 per share, the market capitalisation of the company is Rs. 200 crores. Market capitalisation is one of the most important characteristics that help investors find out the quantum of risk and return in a share.

Portfolio

A portfolio is simply the collection of all the investments an investor has made. We can have as few as one stock in a portfolio, but we can also own an infinite amount of stocks or other securities and assets. It is very important to have right kind of portfolio in place to get good return from the market. Portfolio building has to be done considering many criteria that an investor has planned in terms of getting return from the market.

Intraday Trading

Intraday trading is about buying and selling stocks on the same day so that all positions are closed before trading hours are over on that day.

Dividends

A dividend is a part of the profit distributed by a company among its shareholders. When a company earns profit during

> *"Whether we're talking about socks or stocks, I like buying quality merchandise when it is marked down." – Warren Buffett*

a financial year, a part of that profit is usually distributed as dividends among its shareholders. They can be issued in the form of cash, stocks, or any other form that the company chooses. A number of companies offer dividends to their shareholders. However, it is not necessary that a company will give dividends even if it makes a profit. Many companies reinvest their profits back into the business itself for growth and expansion.

Overvalued stock

When a stock is said to be overvalued, it means that the current price of the stock is considered to be higher than what it should be. We can find out whether a stock is overvalued through certain mathematical metrics such as the Price-to-Earnings ratio. If a stock is considered to be overvalued, the price of the stock is expected to dropdown in Future.

Undervalued stock

An undervalued stock is the opposite of an overvalued stock. It means that a stock is being traded at a value that is lower than its intrinsic value. For example, imagine that the intrinsic value of a stock is Rs. 100 but it is being traded at Rs. 50/share. Investors try to acquire these stocks to get higher returns in the future at a lower cost of investment.

"You don't need to be a rocket scientist. Investing is not a game where the guy with the 160 IQ beats the guy with 130 IQ." – Warren Buffett

Market Breadth

Market breadth is a ratio used in technical analysis to compare the total number of stocks that are rising against the total number of stocks that are falling. The purpose of this technique is to analyze the overall direction in which the stock market is moving.

The formula is as follows:

Market breadth = total number of rising stocks/total number of falling stocks

If the ratio is greater than one, it indicates a positive sentiment or that the market is bullish. A value of less than one means negative sentiment or a bearish market.

Support/Resistance

When it comes to trading in the stock market, the concept of support and resistance are very popular. The concept tells that when the price of a stock reaches a specific predetermined level, it tends to stop and move in the opposite direction. The upper level is known as the resistance and the lower level is known as support.

In case the resistance level is breached at some point, the stock tends to rise in value until it hits another resistance level.

"The markets generally are unpredictable, so that one has to have different scenarios. The idea that you can actually predict what's going to happen contradicts my way of looking at the market."
– George Soros

Benchmark

A benchmark is a standard against which any stock's performance can be measured. There are different benchmarks available to help us to get a good idea of any given stock's performance. Market indices like BSE Sensex and NSE Nifty are a couple of well-known benchmarks.

Averaging Down

When an investor buys more of a stock as the price goes down is termed as averaging down. This makes our cost of purchase per share to get reduced. We might use this strategy if we believe that the consensus about a company is wrong, so we expect the stock price to rebound later.

Beta

A measurement of the relationship between the price of a stock and the movement of the whole market. If stock XYZ has a beta of 1.5, that means that for every 1 point move in the market, stock XYZ moves 1.5 points.

Blue Chip Stocks

Blue-chip stocks offer a stable record of significant dividend payments and have a reputation for sound fiscal management.

"Individual who cannot master their emotions are ill suited to profit from investment process" – Benjamin Graham

Investment to Blue chip Stocks is considered as safe and secure to a great extent. The expression is thought to have been derived from blue gambling chips, which is the highest denomination of chips used in casinos.

Broker

A person who buys or sells an investment option for us in exchange for a fee (a commission).

Open

Open refers to the time at which people can begin trading on a particular exchange.

Close

The close simply refers to the time at which a stock exchange closes to trading.

Execution

When an order to buy or sell has been completed we can say that, the trader has executed the transaction. If we put in an order to sell 1000 shares and if tranaction is done, this means that all 1000 shares have been sold (i.e executed).

"Wall Street is the only place that people ride to in a Rolls Royce to get advice from those who take the subway." – Warren Buffett

Haircut

In the simplest stock market terms, a haircut is an extremely thin spread between the bid and ask prices of a given stock. It can also refer to a situation in which a stock price gets reduced by a specific percentage for margin trades or other purposes.

High

A high refers to a market milestone in which a stock or index reaches a greater price point than previously. Record highs can signal that a stock or index has never reached the current price point, but there are also time-constrained highs, such as 52-week highs.

Low

Low is the opposite of high. It represents a lower price point for a stock or index.

Trend

The general direction in which the stock market (or even an individual share) moves is known as a trend.

For example, if the market has been rising for the past month, we say that the market is on an upward trend. And if it is going down, the market has a downward trend. There is no specific

"If you're in the luckiest 1% of humanity, you owe it to the rest of humanity to think about the other 99%." – Warren Buffett

time limit for a trend. A trend can happen for the short term, the medium term, or even the long term.

Leverage

When we use leverage, we borrow shares in stock from our broker intending to increase our profit. If we borrow shares and sell them all at a higher price point, we return the shares and keep the difference. It is good not to use Leverage unless and untill we are too sure about our trade or investment.

Margin

Margin is the money borrowed from a brokerage firm to purchase an investment. It is the difference between the total value of securities held in an investor's account and the loan amount from the broker. Buying on margin is the act of borrowing money to buy securities. The practice includes buying an asset where the buyer pays only a percentage of the asset's value and borrows the rest from the bank or broker. The broker acts as a lender and the securities in the investor's account act as collateral.

Moving Average

A stock's average price-per-share during a specific period of time is called its moving average. Some common time frames

"In the world of business, the people who are most successful are those who are doing what they love." – Warren Buffett

to study in terms of a stock's moving average include 50 - and 200-day moving averages.

Pink Sheet Stocks/Penny Stocks

The term **"pink sheets"** refers most commonly to **penny stocks**, which are traded at a very low price. They're also called over-the-counter stocks. Trading such shares are considered too risky and trading of such shares is to be avoided by working professionals.

Rally

A rapid increase in the general price level of the market or of the price of a stock is known as a rally. Depending on the overall environment, it might be called a bull rally or a bear rally.

Sector

A group of stocks that are in the same industry belongs to the same sector. Like IT Technology sector, will include TCS, Wipro, Infosys, Tech Mahindra, and other similar companies. Some investors prefer to trade in a specific sector, such as, IT, Pharma, Energy etc. because they know the industry well and can better predict stock price fluctuations. Some prefer to diversify their investment in different sectors and invest accordingly.

"One of the funny things about the stock market is that every time one person buys, another sells, and both think they are astute."
– William Feather

Short Selling

When we short-sell a stock, we borrow shares from someone else with the promise to return them later. We then sell the stock for a profit. It's a way to take advantage of a stock that we believe will decrease in price. After we sell short, we can buy back the shares at a lower price point and take the difference in price as our profit. If we buy at a higher price, we make loss on the differential price.

Volatility

The price movements of a stock or the stock market as a whole represents its volatility. Highly volatile stocks have extreme daily up and down movements and wide intraday trading ranges. Stocks with high volatility are considered for short term investments also.

Yield

Yield refers to the measure of the return on an investment that is received from the payment of a dividend. This is determined by dividing the annual dividend amount by the price paid for the stock. If we bought stock XYZ for 40 per share and it pays a 1.00-per-year dividend, we have a "yield" of 2.5 percent.

"The mutual fund industry has been built, in a sense, on witchcraft."
– Jack Bogle

Bonus Shares

As the word indicates, bonus shares are extra or additional shares that a company gives to its shareholders at no additional cost. The number of bonus shares we get depends on the number of shares we originally own.

For example, imagine that we own a 100 shares of company XYZ. Now, if the company announces a 2:1 bonus, we get 2 shares free for every 1 Share. That is, we would get 200 free shares and our total holding will be 300 shares.

Current Ratio

This ratio indicates a firm's liquidity position. A company with a high current ratio can better meet its short-term liabilities.

In other words, the company has enough back-up, and its day-to-day workings will not be affected due to the pressure of working capital. This ratio is arrived at by dividing current assets with current liabilities.

Defensive Stock

These stocks offers stable earning and consistent dividends irrespective of the nature of the stock market. A defensive stock is also known as a non-cyclical stock.

"Never give up, for that is just the place and time that the tide will turn." – Harriet Beecher Stow

Defensive stocks have generally a beta of less than 1. Having them in our portfolio protects the corpus from eroding in a recession or during market crash to an extent. Generally they don't generate high returns, but they provide regular dividends and generally constant growth also.

Delta

Delta is the ratio that compares the change in the price of the asset to the corresponding change in the price of its derivative. It can be positive or negative depending on the option's time. For the call option, it ranges between 0–1, while for the put option it ranges from −1 to 0.

This is because, in a call option as the price of the underlying asset increases, the option also increases its price. On the other hand, input option as the price increases, the value of the option decreases.

Debt-to-Equity (D/E) Ratio

This ratio tells how much outside funding is used by the company to run its operations as against its funds. Generally, the lower the debt-to-Equity (D/E) ratio, the better it is.

This ratio is arrived at by dividing the total liabilities by total shareholder's Equity. We can easily find this ratio in a company's balance sheet.

"Hope is bogus emotion that only costs you money." – Jim Cramer

Hedge

Hedge refers to a strategy to reduce the risk of the adverse price movement of assets, which can erode the gains of our portfolio.

To make meaningful gains from stock markets, and the fact that they are volatile, we must have this strategy in place to preserve the gains made over the years.

FII

FII' stands for 'foreign institutional investor,' and refers to an investment fund or an investor who puts their money into a country's assets while being headquartered outside. In India, this is a commonly used term to refer to outside entities contributing to the country's financial markets by investing.

Major FIIs for India include hedge funds, pension funds, international insurance companies, and mutual funds, all of which aren't India-based.

DII

'DII' stands for 'domestic institutional investors.' Unlike FIIs, DIIs are investors that invest in the financial assets and securities of the country they are currently residing in.

"Don't test the depth of the river with both your feet while taking the risk" – Warren Buffett

Major DIIs are Indian mutual funds, local pension schemes, Indian insurance companies, and banks or financial institutions.

Retail Investor

A retail investor, also known as an individual investor, is a non-professional investor. Retail investors execute their trades through traditional or online brokerage firms or other types of investment accounts. Retail investors purchase securities for their accounts and often trade in dramatically smaller amounts as compared to institutional investors.

Piotroski Score

The score is named after Stanford accounting Professor Piotroski. The Piotroski Score is a discrete score between zero and nine that reflects nine criteria used to determine the strength of a firm's financial position. The score is used to determine the best value stocks, with nine being the best and zero being the worst.

The score is calculated based on 9 criteria divided into 3 groups.
- Profitability
- Leverage, Liquidity and Source of Funds
- Operating Efficiency

The desire for constant action irrespective of underlying conditions is responsible for many losses in Wall Street." – Jesse Livermore

Profitability

1. Return on Assets (1 point if it is positive in the current year, 0 otherwise);

2. Operating Cash Flow (1 point if it is positive in the current year, 0 otherwise);

3. Change in Return of Assets (ROA) (1 point if ROA is higher in the current year compared to the previous one, 0 otherwise);

4. Accruals (1 point if Operating Cash Flow/Total Assets is higher than ROA in the current year, 0 otherwise);

Leverage, Liquidity and Source of Funds

1. Change in Leverage (long-term) ratio (1 point if the ratio is lower this year compared to the previous one, 0 otherwise);

2. Change in Current ratio (1 point if it is higher in the current year compared to the previous one, 0 otherwise);

3. Change in the number of shares (1 point if no new shares were issued during the last year);

Operating Efficiency

1. Change in Gross Margin (1 point if it is higher in the current year compared to the previous one, 0 otherwise);

The trend is your friend until the end when it bends." – Ed Seykota

2. Change in Asset Turnover ratio (1 point if it is higher in the current year compared to the previous one, 0 otherwise);

A company gets 1 point for each met criteria. Summing up of all achieved points gives Piotroski Score (number between 0 and 9).

Stock Market Indices

There are thousands of companies listed on stock markets, making it almost impossible to monitor each company and to ascertain the direction of Stock market. This is why stock market indices are created with limited number of stocks to bring together a select group of reputed company stocks and regularly measures them to show the performance of the overall market or a certain segment of the market.

In short, an index helps investors understand the health of the stock market, and enables them to study the market sentiment, and makes it easy to compare the performance of an individual stock.

In India the Sensex and Nifty-50 are two popular benchmark indices that largely reflect the performance of the Bombay Stock Exchange (BSE) and National Stock Exchange (NSE).

"Never confuse your position with your best interest. Many traders take a position in a stock and form an emotional attachment to it. They'll start losing money, and instead of stopping themselves out, they'll find brand new reasons to stay in. When in doubt, get out!" – Jeff Cooper

To understand how each sector of the stock market is doing, there are sectoral indices such as Nifty Bank. Nifty Auto etc.

Bombay Stock Exchange

Bombay Stock Exchange is generally known as BSE Sensex. It is the oldest stock index in India; it is a collection of 30 actively traded stocks in the BSE that represent a cross-section of all industries in India. 100 was taken as the base value of this index on 1st April 1979.

This market-weighted free-float BSE Sensex is considered as the stock market pulse in India that is used extensively in BSE trading.

NSE Nifty

Nifty, also known as NIFTY 50 is the stock market index of the National Stock Exchange (NSE), the leading stock exchange of India. This index comprises 50 traded stocks from different sectors based on their capitalization. These cover the major 22 sectors of the Indian economy and provide a wide exposure to the Indian financial market that investment managers can look at. The rise and fall of the NIFTY depend on the price movement of the stocks that it contains and acts as a guide of the capital market in India. There are some common stocks between BSE and NSE trading.

The core problem, however, is the need to fit markets into a style of trading rather than finding ways to trade that fit with market behavior." – Brett Steenbarger

Some Important World Indices are

Dow Jones

The Dow Jones Industrial Average (DJIA), also known as the Dow 30, is a stock market index that tracks 30 large, publicly-owned blue-chip companies trading on the New York Stock Exchange (NYSE) and the NASDAQ

Nasdaq

The NASDAQ Composite is a stock market index that includes the stocks listed on the NASDAQ stock market. Along with the Dow Jones Industrial Average and S&P 500 Index, it is one of the three most-followed stock market indices in the United States. The composition of the NASDAQ Composite is heavily weighted towards companies in the information technology sector.

S&P 500

The S&P 500 Index or the Standard & Poor's 500 Index is a market-capitalization-weighted index of 500 of the largest publicly-traded companies in the U.S. It is not an exact list of the top 500 U.S. companies by market capitalization. The index is widely regarded as the best gauge of large-cap U.S. equities.

"Stock price movements actually begin to reflect new developments before it is generally recognized that they have taken place." – Arthur Zeikel

MSCI

The MSCI Emerging Markets Index stands for Morgan Stanley Capital International (MSCI) and is an index used to measure Stock market performance in global emerging markets. MSCI Emerging Market Index captures mid and large caps across more than two dozen emerging market countries.

The MSCI Emerging Markets Index consists of developing economies including Argentina, Brazil, Chile, China, Colombia, Czech Republic, Egypt, Greece, Hungary, India, Indonesia, Korea, Malaysia, Mexico, Pakistan, Peru, Philippines, Poland, Qatar, Russia, Saudi Arabia, South Africa, Taiwan, Thailand, Turkey, and the United Arab Emirates.

Nikkei

The Nikkei is Japan's Nikkei 225 Stock Average, the leading and most-respected index of Japanese stocks. It is a price-weighted index composed of Japan's top 225 blue-chip companies traded on the Tokyo Stock Exchange.

Some of the best-known companies listed in the Nikkei are Sony Corporation, Canon Inc, Nissan Motor Company, and Honda Motor Company.

"Your success in investing will depend in part on your character and guts, and in part on your ability to realize at the height of ebullience and the depth of despair alike that this too shall pass." – John C. Bogle

Hang Seng (HSI)

The Hang Seng Index or HSI is a market capitalization-weighted index of the largest companies that trade on the Hong Kong Exchange.

The Hang Seng Index (HSI) is a free-float-adjusted market-capitalization-weighted stock-market index in Hong Kong. It is used to record and monitor daily changes of the largest companies of the Hong Kong stock market and is the main indicator of the overall market performance in Hong Kong

FTSE 100

The Financial Times Stock Exchange Group (FTSE), also known by the nickname of "Footsie," is an independent organization. It is similar to Standard & Poor's, which specializes in creating index offerings for the global financial markets. An index will represent a market segment and is a hypothetical portfolio of stock holdings. The most well-known index, among many at FTSE, is the FTSE 100, which is composed of blue-chip stocks listed on the London Stock Exchange. European Indices are Dax (Germany), CAC 40 (France)

Finding the best person or the best organization to invest your money is one of the most important financial decisions you'll ever make.
– Bill Gross

2.2 Stock Market – Products

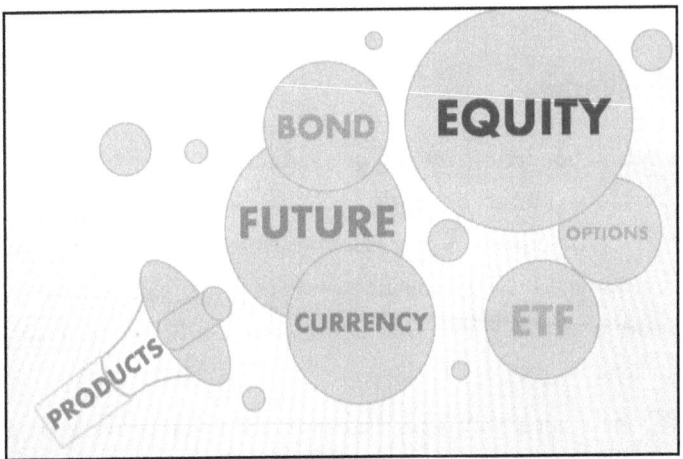

There are different products available in the stock market and they can be divided into 3 asset classes for trading:

- Capital market for the listing and trading of Equities
- Derivative Market
- Fixed income Bond/securities

Equity and Linked Products

Equity and Equity-linked products available for trading in the cash market which includes stocks, Indices, International

"In trading the impossible happens about twice a year." – Henri M Simoes

Depository Receipts (IDRs), Exchange Traded Funds (ETFs), and Mutual Fund schemes.

Stock represents the ownership of portions of the future earnings potential of the firm. This is why projections of future performance can have a significant influence on daily stock trading prices.

Derivative

Under the derivatives segment, different exchanges offers derivative contract on Stock, Indices, Currency, Interest Rates, and Commodities. A derivative is a financial instrument that derives its value from the movement or performance of one or many underlying assets like stocks, commodities, bonds, and currency.

All these assets which can be considered as "underlying" to a derivative product are subject to change in value. A feature that is common to all assets is the risk that they carry for the change in the value. The Derivative contracts seek to transfer these risks from a counterparty that is not comfortable with the risk to one that is.

There are two major specific derivative products namely are Futures and Options.

> *"The game of speculation is the most uniformly fascinating game in the world. But it is not a game for the stupid, the mentally lazy, the person of inferior emotional balance, or the get-rich-quick adventurer. They will die poor."* – Jesse Livermore

Fixed Income Securities

Fixed income refers to those types of investment security that pay investors fixed interest or dividend payments until its maturity date.

At maturity, investors are repaid the principal amount they had invested.

The fixed income securities and Debt products include Negotiated Trade Reporting in Government securities, Sovereign Gold Bonds, Corporate Bonds, and other debt securities traded on multiple platforms.

Fixed-Income securities are debt instruments that pay a fixed amount of interest payments to the investors. The interest payments are typically made semiannually or annually while the principal invested returns to the investor at maturity. Bonds are the most common form of fixed-income securities

Following is the major difference between Stock/Share and Fixed Income Security.

Stock/Share	Fixed Income
Are Share Owners	Considered as Creditors
Claim Profit	Claim Loaned Amount and Interest as agreed.
High Risk and High Return Instrument	Low Risk and Low Return instrument

"Dangers of watching every tick are twofold: overtrading and increased chances of prematurely liquidating good positions"
– Jack Schwager

Issued by Corporates as Shares	Issued by Govt./Financial institutions or Corporates
Last claim on an asset in case of bankruptcy	Has priority over Stock Holders
The dividend is paid on the earning.	No Dividend
Stock holders Enjoy Voting Rights	Have No Voting Rights

"Diversify. But carve out 10 to 20 percent for the most unloved part of the market: emerging markets value." – Robert D. Arnott

2.3 Products and Associated Risks

Below three products are widely used for investment. There are different levels of risks associated with these products. Since this book is written keeping the salaried people, in particular, it is recommended to invest in Stock/Stock Segment as it provides High Returns for High Risk associated. The High Risk is to be managed and mitigated with knowledge and the right investment strategies which will reduce the risk and help increase the return on investment.

"Derivatives are financial weapons of mass destruction."
– Warren Buffett

Derivative Products is to be avoided till we are not comfortable investing in Stock delivery instrument. Derivative leads to erosion of capital very fast in case it is not traded properly. So Derivative is to be avoided till we are confident of investing in it.

Product	Risk Associated	Remarks
Stock/Shares	High Risk and High Returns	Hard-earned money can be invested with all possible risk mitigation strategies. Long terms investment gives good returns.
Fixed Income	Low-Risk Low Returns	Hard earned money can be invested.
Derivatives	Very High Risk and Very High Returns	Investment of hard-earned money is to be avoided. This instrument can be used for hedging.

"Money is made by conservative trading rather than by the effort to get large profits by taking large risks." – Charles Dow

2.4 Advantages of Investing in Stock Market

Working professionals invest their hard earned money and hence erosion of the capital invested is not expected or desired at any cost. Hence it is suggested to stay away from derivatives till we are very confident of investing in them after having acquired sufficient knowledge for investing in this instrument. The other two options, fixed income and Stock market, are better options to invest for working professionals. Fixed Income instrument gives fixed income as agreed, whereas

"Trading doesn't just reveal your character, it also builds it if you stay in the game long enough." – Yvan Byeajee

the Stock Market gives high returns if the associated risks are managed and mitigated properly.

Investment in Stock/Shares is suggested for the following reasons:-

If Rewarded, Returns are Higher

Stock Market provides a high return on investment and is a relatively safe mode of investment. It allows us to keep the share as long as we want to maximize the profit. There is always an exit route if someone wants to sell the Stock on any day.

The Exponential Growth of Funds is Possible

There are many stocks that have given exponential growth to the shareholders and there will be many in the future. Picking the right stocks gives a possibility to high and exponential growth on the investment.

Market Fluctuations and Randomness can be Taken up as an Advantage

The stock market is volatile and this makes it very exciting. Volatility and randomness of the market gives the opportunity to earn money if the right risk management strategies are put in place and followed. Some of the investors who follow the

"The process by which one accumulates money is so simple, yet so hard to implement for most." – Yvan Byeajee

strategy of making small but frequent profit booking, always try to encash the volatility of the market for booking the profit. Market fluctuation also provides an opportunity to buy at less and sell at high, the opportunity that everyone is looking for in the stock market.

Provides Dividend, in Addition to the Growth of the Fund

Shareholders get a dividend from the companies, based on the earnings of the company. There are many high dividend-paying companies and investment in such companies is preferred by investors.

A dividend is the distribution of some of a company's earnings to a class of its shareholders. However, they may also be paid in additional shares of stock.

Option to Invest in the Primary and Secondary Stock Market

In a primary market, securities are created for the first time for investors to purchase. New securities are issued in this market through a stock exchange, enabling the companies to raise capital through IPO (Initial Public Offering).

There is an option to invest in the secondary Stock market if we miss the opportunity to invest in the primary market.

"I just wait until there is money lying in the corner, and all I have to do is go over there and pick it up. I do nothing in the meantime."
— Jim Rogers

The secondary market is the financial market in which previously issued financial instruments such as stock, bonds, are sold. In the secondary market, investors buy and sell securities from other investors.

Knowledge gain

We always gain knowledge when we plan to invest in the right company, as we have to do research before investing.

So, when we start investing, we understand why we are investing, when to buy and sell, understand the big picture of the market, and understand different strategies of the market.

We need not be an expert in the stock market to start investing. Through gradual and systematic learning, we can become an expert in due course of time. As it is said, **"Knowledge is Power"**, reading a lot about the stock market utilizing articles, books, videos, etc. will help inculcate the required skill set to begin our investment journey.

Fall Back Strategy in Case of Urgent Fund Requirement

Since exit from any Stock and the Stock Market is easy, it is always a source for reaching the fund requirement in case of exigencies.

"I have two basic rules about winning in trading as well as in life: 1. If you don't bet, you can't win. 2. If you lose all your chips, you can't bet." – Larry Hite

Although it is recommended to remain invested for long term gain, it is sometimes imperative to get the fund back to meet some urgent requirements. In such scenarios, the investment gives a good option and we can sell our profit-making stocks to get the fund requirement met.

"In life and business, there are two cardinal sins. The first is to act precipitously without thought and the second is to not act at all."
– Carl Icahn

2.5 Important Ratios and Things to Know Before Investing

The most difficult component of any investment is to find the right stock to invest in. To identify the right stock, the fundamentals of the Company is to be looked into.

There are various indicators that indicate the Company's fundamentals and some of the important ones are listed below:

"The obvious rarely happens, the unexpected constantly occurs."
– Jesse Livermore

Market Capitalization

Market capitalization is one of the most effective ways of evaluating the market value of a company. Since it represents the "market" value of a company, it is computed based on the current market price (CMP) of its shares and the total number of outstanding shares. Market cap is also used to compare and categorize the size of companies among investors and analysts. Generally, companies are categorized as Large-, Mid-, or Small-cap depending on their market capitalization. Blue chip companies are often large-cap while the very smallest are referred to micro-caps companies.

Large-Cap companies are businesses that are well-established and have a significant market share. Large-cap companies have market caps of INR 20,000 crore plus. These companies are particularly more stable and dominate the industry in their segment. They hold themselves well in times of recession or during other negative events like a pandemic or market crash or similar kind of situation. Also, they have a long past and usually have been functioning for decades with good reputations. Large-cap stocks are a good option if we want less risk on our investment. These stocks are generally less volatile in comparison to mid-cap and small-cap stocks. The lower volatility makes them less risky.

Reliance Industries, TCS, HDFC Bank, Infosys, Hindustan Unilever are examples of some large-cap market companies

"Stocks are bought not in fear but in hope. They are typically sold out of fear." – Justin Mamis

that are listed on the stock exchanges of India. Their strong foothold in the market and consistent good performance make them good choices for long-term investors.

Mid-cap companies are companies whose market cap is above INR 5,000 crore but less than INR 20,000 crore. Investing in these companies can be riskier than investing in large-cap market companies. Mid-caps tend to be more volatile and also these can turn into large-cap companies in the long run. These companies offer a higher growth potential than large-cap companies. Due to high vitality and high returns, investors are attracted to investing in mid-cap companies.

Torrent Power, Endurance Tech., Amara Raja Batteries, Godrej Agrovet, Aegis Logistics, Granules India, Astra Zeneca, ERIS Lifescience, Vinati Organics, Dixon Technologies (India) Ltd, Apollo Tyre, Akzo Nobel, Affle India are some examples of Mid-cap companies that are listed on the stock exchanges of India.

Small-cap companies have a market capitalization of less than INR 5,000 crore. These companies are relatively smaller in size and have significant growth potential. Their low probability for success makes them risky but they give very good returns over long term if successful. The stocks of these companies are very volatile and hence making high losses and profit are possible with these small-cap stocks. When the economy is emerging out of a recession, small-cap stocks turn out to be outperformers most of the time.

"Only The Game, Can Teach You The Game" – Jesse Livermore

eClerx Services, Caplin Point Lab, Suprajit Engineering Ltd., Dhanuka Agritech, Advanced Enzyme., J K Tyre, Tata Steel Long Product, IRB Infra, Borosil renewables Ltd, Ashoka Buildcon are some examples of small-cap market companies that are listed on the stock exchanges of India.

The Financials

Stock Market investors need not learn an incredible amount for analyzing a company's financial statements. The company's income statement, balance sheet, and statement of cash flows are strikingly useful in understanding how a company functions, its stability, and how much its stock is worth.

Publicly traded companies provide financial statements quarterly to the Securities and Exchange Commission and are available on different securities websites for reference.

Uncover the income statement on the website and analyze the trends in top-line sales, expenses, and bottom-line income. Growing sales and earnings are excellent indicators, but declining sales, declining earnings, and increasing expenses suggest the company is struggling and maybe a high-risk option from an investment perspective. So, the sale, expenses, profitability are very important parameters to check out, before making any investment decision on any stock.

Further analyze the balance sheet. Ascertain if the company has paid off or increased its debt. Analyze the cash flow statement

"He who knows when he can fight and when he cannot will be victorious." – Sun Tzu

of the company and also different ratios which gives indication on the financial health or growth of the company.

Price to Earnings Ratio - PE Ratio

PE = Share Price/EPS

The price-to-earnings ratio (P/E) is one of the most widely used metrics by investors and analysts to determine stock valuation. In addition to showing whether a company's stock price is overvalued or undervalued, the P/E can indicate how a stock's valuation relates to its peer group companies and sector average.

The P/E ratio helps investors determine the market value of a stock as compared to the company's earnings. In short, the P/E shows what the market is willing to pay today for a stock.

However, companies that grow faster than average, typically have higher P/Es, such as emerging technology companies or companies which have launched some new concept or product which the market is accepting well. A higher P/E ratio shows that investors are willing to pay a higher share price today, possibly because of growth expectations of the company in the future. A high P/E does not necessarily mean a stock is overvalued. Investors not only use the P/E ratio to determine a stock's market value but also in determining future earnings growth.

A high P/E could also mean that a stock's price is high relative to earnings and possibly overvalued. Conversely, a low P/E

"Amateurs think about how much money they can make. Professionals think about how much money they could lose." – Jack Schwager

might indicate that the current stock price is low relative to earnings and there is scope of rise further.

P/E Ratio is an important ratio and is to be referred before investing in any stock, but is not the only indicator that needs to be referred for making decision on investment.

Some Stocks with High P/E TTM (Mar 2021)

S.No.	Company Name	PE (TTM)	Sector - PE
1	Jubilant Woodworks	254.39	70.06
2	Apollo Hospital Enterprises	198.45	71.05
3	Zydus Wellness	220.16	72.02
4	Minda Industries	184.2	84.46
5	Titan Company	173.23	68.53

Some Stocks with Low P/E TTM (Mar 2021)

S.No.	Company Name	PE (TTM)	Sector - PE
1	Godrej Agrovet	28.83	70.06
2	Tata Coffee	23.88	67.99
3	Finolex Industries	16.41	65.81
4	CCL Products	19.4	67.99
5	Hindalco Industries Ltd	34.13	114.3

EPS – Earning Per Share

EPS indicates how much money a company makes for each share of its stock, and is a widely used metric to estimate

"All the math you need in the stock market you get in the fourth grade." – Peter Lynch

Things to Know Before Investing

corporate value. In other words, EPS measures how much of the company's profit can be allocated to each share of stock.

The higher the EPS, the better is the stock.

EPS is a ratio, which divides net earnings available to common shareholders by the average outstanding shares over a certain time period. The EPS formula indicates a company's competency to produce net profits for common shareholders.

A single EPS value for one company may not indicate the right inference. The number is more valuable when compared and analyzed against other companies in the industry, and when compared to the company's share price (the P/E Ratio). Between two companies in the same industry with the same number of shares outstanding, higher EPS indicates better profitability. EPS is typically used in conjunction with a company's share price to determine whether it is relatively "cheap" (low P/E ratio) or "expensive" (high P/E ratio).

Following are the EPS (TTM) for Agrochemicals Company (Mar 2021)

Sr. #	**Company Name**	Sector	EPS (TTM)
1	UPL	Agro Chemicals	31.74
2	Sharda Cropchem	Agro Chemicals	26.26
3	Dhanuka Agritech	Agro Chemicals	43.14
4	Rallis India	Agro Chemicals	11.37
5	PI Ind	Agro Chemicals	44.11

"Don't test the depth of the river with both your feet while taking the risk" – *Warren Buffett*

Profit Margin TTM (Trailing Twelve Months)

Profit margin is one of the frequently used profitability ratios to gauge the degree to which a company or a business entity makes money. It represents what percentage of sales has turned into profits. Simply put, the percentage figure indicates how much profit the business has generated against sales generated.

Debt Equity D/E Ratio

The debt-to-Stock (D/E) ratio is calculated by dividing a company's total liabilities by its shareholder Stock. The ratio is used to evaluate a company's financial leverage.

The D/E ratio is an important metric used in corporate finance.

It is a measure of the degree to which a company is financing its operations through debt versus wholly-owned funds. It reflects the ability of shareholder Stock to cover all outstanding debts in the event of a business downturn.

Return on Equity – ROE

Return on Equity (ROE) is a measure of financial performance and is calculated by dividing net income by shareholders' Equity. Because shareholders' Equity is equal to a company's assets minus its debt, ROE is considered the return on net assets. ROE is considered a measure of the profitability of a corporation concerning stockholders' Equity.

"In order to succeed, you first have to be willing to experience failure."
– *Yvan Byeajee*

Net income is calculated before dividends are paid to common shareholders and after dividends are paid to preferred shareholders and interest to lenders.

Return on Equity = Net Income/Average Shareholders' Equity

Return On Capital Employed - ROCE

It is a financial ratio that determines a company's profitability and the efficiency of the capital deployed. A higher ROCE implies a more economical use of capital.

The ROCE should be higher than the capital cost. If not, the company is less productive.

ROCE Formula

ROCE = EBIT/Capital Employed.

EBIT = Earnings Before Interest and Tax
Capital Employed = Total Assets – Current Liabilities.

Calculating Return on Capital Employed is a useful means of comparing profits across companies based on the amount of capital. It is insufficient to look at the EBIT alone to determine which company is a better for investment. We also have to look at the capital and calculate the ROCE. Many consider ROCE a more reliable formula than ROE for calculating a company's future earnings because of current liabilities and expenses.

Below are some examples with Data(Mar 2021)

"Trade the market for what it is, not for what you trust it to be."

SR #	Company Name	Sector	ROE (%)	ROCE (%)
1	Tata Motors	Auto	-19.13	-0.25
2	Bajaj Auto	Auto	24.06	28.63
3	Eicher Motors	Auto	18.3	22.46
4	Hero Motocorp	Auto	25.25	25.62
5	TVS Motor Co.	Auto	19.03	19.14
6	Ashok Leyland	Auto	4.32	11.1
7	Mahindra and Mahindra	Auto	0.31	7.65
8	Maruti Suzuki India Ltd.	Auto	11.4	13.6

Compounded Annual Growth Rate

Compound Annual Growth Rate (CAGR) is a measure of the average yearly growth of our investments over a certain time period. It tells you the average rate of return we have earned on our investments every year. CAGR is very useful for investors because it is an accurate measure of investment growth (or fall) over time.

CAGR = (Ending balance/Beginning balance)$^{1/n}$ - 1

Here,

Ending balance is the value of the investment at the end of the investment period Beginning balance is the value of the investment at the beginning of the period

N is the number of years for which you have invested

"For investors as a whole, returns decrease as motion increases."
– Warren Buffett,

Dividend Yield

A stock's dividend yield tells us how much dividend income we receive in comparison to the current price of the stock. Acquiring stocks with a high dividend yield can provide a good source of income.

Dividend Yield = Dividend per share/Market value per share.

Below are some of the Examples for Dividend Yield for Cement Sector (Data – Mar 2021).

Sr #	Company Name	Sector	Dividend Yield
1	Ambuja Cements	Cement	0.55
2	Ultra Tech	Cement	0.2
3	Shree Cement	Cement	0.41
4	ACC	Cement	0.81
5	Ramco Cement	Cement	0.29
6	Prism Johnson Ltd	Cement	1.02
7	J K Cement	Cement	0.28
8	Sh Digvijay Cement	Cement	2.68
9	Heidelberg Cement	Cement	3.3

"In trading, you can't stop loss from happening but you can avoid big loss by using stop loss in your trades." – Olawale Daniel

2.6 Sectors – Its Performance and Analysis

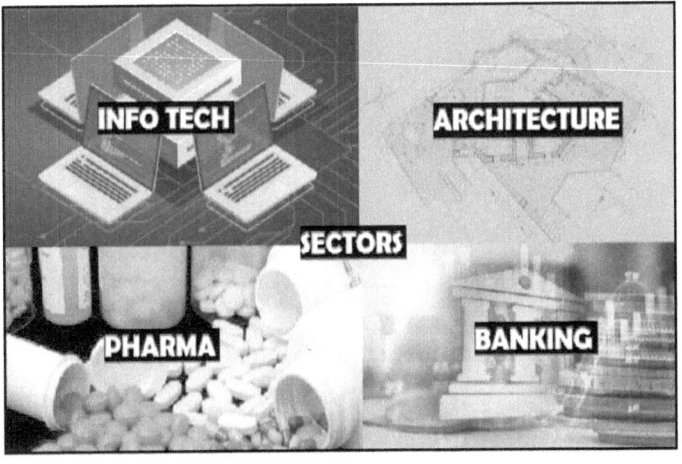

We analyze the latest trend in major sectors by tracking the change in market-cap of individual sectors for a different period, daily, quarterly, monthly, half-yearly, and year-to-date.

The advance-decline ratio (ADR) is a technical indicator used to assess stock market sentiment. The ratio compares the number of stocks that increased in value to the number of stocks that decreased in value. In other words, the ADR

"Sheer will and determination is no substitute for something that actually works." – *Jason Klatt*

compares the number of stocks that rose in price versus the number of stocks that declined in price.

The formula for Advance Decline Ratio

ADR = Number of Advancing Stock/Number of declining Stock

Where:

Number of Advancing Stocks refers to the number of stocks that increased in value; and

Number of Declining Stocks refers to the number of stocks that declined in value.

The ratio can be used for any desired timeframe. For example, ADR can be for one day, a one-month period, or for one year.

The A/D ratio can be interpreted in several ways:

- A ratio that increases over time is thought to signal a bullish market trend, while a ratio that is decreasing is thought to signal a bearish trend.

- A relatively high ratio can indicate an overbought market, one that is ready for a near term decline.

- A relatively low ratio can signal an oversold market, that is ready for a near term increase.

Major Sectors

Following are some of the major sectors in Share Market. There are many more sectors which can be explored by the readers for study and analysis.

"You can lose your opinion of you can lose your money." – Adam Grimes

IT - Consulting & Software	Finance	Pharmaceuticals
Consumer Goods - Electricals	Plastic	Consumer/Electronics
Hospital and Medical Services	Chemical	Food Processing
Power - Generation & Distribution	Paint	Plantation - Tea
Marine Ports & Services	Steel	Tyre and Rubber
Oil & Gas Marketing and Distribution	Cement	Auto Ancillaries
Mining and Metal	Textile	Construction & Engineering
Transport and Logistics	Banking	Housing Finance
Glass and Glass Products	Realty	Breweries & Distilleries
Refineries/Petro Products	Cables	Leather Products/Foot ware
Publishing	Auto	Agro Chemical
Airlines	FMCG	Hotel
Oil & Gas – Exploration and Production	Paper	Miscellaneous
Others………		

Sectors and Its Performance

We will analyses some major sectors and some of the stocks which are more commonly traded in those sectors. We will also analyze some of the parameters and performance of the stocks and sectors so that it gives high level idea on their performance and return on investment these sectors and stocks.

"Cut your losses. Cut your losses. Cut your losses. Then maybe you have a chance." – Ed Seykota

Please note that these are only few stocks of these sectors. Many more Stocks can be analyzed by readers at their end.

Inclusion of all the sectors and theirs Stocks is not done in the book. Only selected sectors and selected stocks are considered and mentioned in this book for high level understanding of the sectors.

The data mentioned in this book are of Month Feb-Mar 2021.

Sales figure considered are of FY 2020.

Knowing the history of any stock/sector helps to predict the future of the stock/sector, although there are many factors which eventually decide the future performance of any stock or sector.

IT - Consulting & Software

Trends of last decade reveals robust wealth creation in IT – Consulting and Software Sector. Also it has set trend in the industry in attracting huge foreign direct investment.

This sector has played a major role in defining the country's economy and has provided employment to millions of people directly and indirectly. The major names in this sector include Tata Consultancy Services (TCS), Infosys, Wipro, Tech Mahindra.

As the world is getting more and more technologically advanced and digitized with new and emerging IT technologies, the future of the sector and the workforce involved holds unlimited possibilities on better and more refined business and growth.

"Take your profits or someone else will take them for you." – J.J. Evans

Things to Know Before Investing

The emerging IT technologies, like Robotic Process Automation, Virtual Reality, Block chain, IOT, IIOT, are the ones that can profoundly impact and transform the entire workforce of the future and present a great scope to drive business outcomes.

Listed here are few of the companies of this sector which can be studied and analyzed by the readers for investment and building their portfolio. Some high level detail of the sector and stocks is described below.

Sr #	Company Name	Piotroski Score	Sales (In Cr) Year 2020
1	TCS	7	156949
2	Infosys	6	90971
3	HCL Technologies	6	70676
4	Wipro	7	61137
5	Tech Mahindra	5	36867
6	L & T Infotech	5	10878
7	Mindtree	5	7764
8	Coforge Limited	4	4183
9	Zensar Tech.	5	4181
10	BirlaSoft	5	3290
11	eClerx Services	6	1437
12	Vakrangee	5	685
13	AXISCADES Technology	7	672
14	NewGen Software Tech	5	660

"Risk comes from not knowing what you are doing." – Warren Buffett

This sectors has small, mid and large market cap companies and most are performing and providing good return on investment.

Also Majority of these companies mentioned above have recorded 3 Year CAGR Positive Revenue and 3 Year CAGR Positive Net Profit indicating good growth of the sectors in terms of sales and profit.

Tata Consultancy Services maintained the Top on Market Capitalization and Sales.

Companies with High market Cap and sales are TCS, Infosys, HCL Technologies, Wipro, L&T Infotech and Tech Mahindra.

Ratio Beta of most of all high turnover companies is less than 1 indicating less risk and volatility for this sector. This sector can be chosen for investment for consistent and regular growth with less risk on investment. PE of most of the stocks mentioned are near to industry PE indicating healthy growth of the sector in the past and there is further possibility of growth of the sector.

Stocks in the provided list above has given excellent return on investment. Excellent return on investment is provided by Birlasoft in last 2 years and Coforge Limited has provided Outstanding Return in last 5 years.

EClerx Services Ltd., Infosys Ltd., Tata Consultancy Services Ltd., have also provided periodic and good return on investment.

"Never let a win go to your head, or a loss to your heart." – Chuck D.

Pharmaceuticals

India enjoys an important position in the global pharmaceuticals sector.

It is the largest provider of generic medicines globally and supplies major global demand for vaccines. India is the only country with largest number of US-FDA compliant Pharma plants outside of USA.

The country is home to more than 3,000 pharmaceutical companies with a strong network of over 10,000 manufacturing facilities.

The country has a large pool of scientists and engineers with a potential to guide the industry ahead to a greater heights. The Medicine spending in India is projected to grow in coming five years, leading India to become one of the top 10 countries in terms of medicine spending. Better growth in domestic sales would also depend on the ability of companies to align their product portfolio towards chronic therapies for diseases which are on the rise in the country and worldwide.

Pharmaceutical Sector stock has provided very good returns on the investment in the past.

Listed here are few of the companies of this sector which can be studied and analyzed by the readers for investment and building their portfolio. Some high level detail of the sector and stocks is described below.

"Some people make shoes. Some people make houses. We make money, and people are willing to pay us a lot to make money for them."
– Monroe Trout

Cruising through the Stock Market

Sr #	Company Name	Piotroski Score	Sales (In Cr) Year 2020
1	Sun Pharma.Inds.	8	32837
2	Aurobindo Pharma	9	23098
3	Dr Reddy's Labs	8	17517
4	Cipla	7	17131
5	Lupin	3	15374
6	Cadila Health.	7	14253
7	Glenmark Pharma.	5	10640
8	Jubilant Pharmova Ltd	7	9154
9	Torrent Pharma	8	7939
10	Divi's Lab.	6	5310
11	Alembic Pharma	5	4605
12	Abbott India	8	4093
13	Abbott India Ltd	8	4093
14	Laurus Labs	8	2831
15	Granules India	9	2598
16	Ajanta Pharma	6	2587
17	Dishman Carbogen Amcis	5	2043
18	Syngene Intl.	7	2011
19	Natco Pharma	4	1915
20	ERIS Lifescience	8	1074
21	Caplin Point Lab	3	863
22	AstraZeneca	8	831

This sectors has small, mid and large market cap companies. Pharmaceutical sectors has performed well in the past.

"It's never too late to learn." – Malcolm Forbes

Company with Highest Market Cap and Sales is Sun Pharma in this sector.

Pharmaceutical sectors has many good high performing companies providing excellent return on investment. In this sector most of the companies have recorded 3 Year CAGR Positive Revenue and 3 Year CAGR Positive Net Profit indicating good growth of the sector.

Ratio - Beta of almost all companies mentioned is less than 1 indicating less risk and volatility making it a relatively safe sector for investment. Many companies with PE less than Industry PE indicating high scope for investment with many stocks which have potential to provide good returns in the future.

Excellent return in the range 40 to 125 percent in last 1 to 2 years on most of the stocks has been observed.

Granules India Limited, Dr Roddy's Laboratories Ltd, Lupin Limited, Divi's Laboratories Limited, Alembic Pharmaceuticals Ltd, Cipla Limited, Jubilant Pharmova Ltd., Aurobindo Pharma Ltd., Eris Lifesciences Ltd have provided good return on investment in last 1 year.

Finance

India's financial sector has been one of the fastest growing sectors in the economy. The economy has witnessed increased private

"Your economic security does not lie in your job; it lies in your power to produce – to think, to learn, to create, to adapt. That's true financial independence. It's not having wealth; it's having the power to produce wealth." – Stephen. R. Covey

sector entry and participation including significant increase in banks, insurance companies, mutual funds, and venture capital and investment institutions in last three decades. The various steps taken by the government and the regulators to meet the challenges of this sectors has ensured the emergence of strong and transparent financial sector. The entry of new players made the existing players more competitive and compelled upgrading their product offerings, services and distribution channels.

This has given an impetus to the financial sector for growth and progress.

Listed here are few of the companies of this sector which can be studied and analyzed by the readers for investment and building their portfolio. Some high level detail of the sector and stocks is described below.

S.No.	Company Name	Piotroski Score	Turnover (In Cr)
1	PFC - Power Finance Corporation	3	62189
2	Bajaj Fin Serve	5	54346
3	Bajaj Finance	3	26373
4	Shriram Transport Finance	2	16562
5	L&T Finance Holding	6	14175
6	Muthoot Finance Ltd	3	9683
7	Manappuram Finance Ltd	3	5465

"Financial peace isn't the acquisition of stuff. It's learning to live on less than you make, so you can give money back and have money to invest. You can't win until you do this." – Dave Ramsey

8	HDFC AMC	6	2003
	(Asset Management Co)		
9	Paisalo Digital Ltd	7	337
10	Dhani Services Ltd	6	305
11	Dolat Investment Ltd	6	87

This sector has all three categories i.e Small Cap, Mid Cap and Large Cap companies.

All above mentioned companies have 3 Year CAGR Positive Revenue and 3 Year CAGR Positive Net Profit indicating growing and performing sector and hence good for investment too.

PFC being is at Top on Turnover and Bajaj Finance is at Top on Market Capitalization

Companies with High market Cap are PFC, Bajaj Finserve, Bajaj Finance, HDFC AMC, Muthoot Finance Ltd.

Ratio Beta is more than 1 for most of the companies indicating high volatility sector and hence short term profit booking can be planned and targeted in this sector. PE of most of the stocks are less than sector PE indicating there is good possibility of growth in this sector.

Excellent return in past two years by Bajaj Finance, HDFC AMC, Muthoot Finance, Dhani Services Ltd and Paisalo Digital. In past five years by Bajaj Finance, Bajaj Finserve, and Manappuram Finance Ltd has provided excellent return in investment.

"When you learn to let go of the need to be right, being wrong gradually lose its power to disturb you." – Yvan Byeajee

Steel

Growth in the steel sector is driven by the demand in the manufacturing, construction and engineering, infrastructure, Auto, Auto Ancillaries and housing. All these sectors are growing leading to the growth of Steel Sector in India.

Today India is among the top producers of Steel in the world and per capita consumption is also on the rise. Govt of India is making different schemes which will push the consumption of Steel in the rural area.

The growth in the Indian steel sector has been supported by domestic availability of raw materials such as iron ore and cost-effective labour. Also the country has many state-of-the-art steel plants which have gone continuous modernization and upgrade to achieve higher operational efficiency levels.

Listed here are few of the companies of this sector which can be studied and analyzed by the readers for investment and building their portfolio. Some high level detail of the sector and stocks is described below.

S.No.	Company Name	Piotroski Score	Sales (In Cr) Year 2020
1	Tata Steel	5	139816
2	JSW Steel	4	73326
3	SAIL	3	61664
4	Jindal Steel & Power Ltd	4	36917

"Losses are necessary, as long as they are associated with a technique to help you learn from them." – David Sikhosana

5	Jindal Stainless (Hisaar) Ltd	8	9397
6	Tata Steel BSL Ltd	4	5881
7	Jindal Stainless Ltd	5	3584
8	Tata Steel Long Product	2	3489
9	JSW Ispat Spl. Prod	3	2638
10	Ratnamani Metals	3	2583

In Steel Sector Companies are in Small, Mid and Large Cap categories.

All Companies have registered 3 Year CAGR Positive Revenue. 3 Year CAGR Positive Net Profit is recorded by Tata Steel, JSW Steel, Tata steel Long Product, Jindal Steel, Ratnamani Metals.

Tata Steel being has the highest Last Year Sales whereas JSW steel has maintained top position on Market Capitalization.

Ratio Beta is more than 1 for most of the companies indicating high volatility sector and hence short term profit booking can be planned and targeted in this sector. PE Ratio is mix where many are above and many are below the Sector PE indicating there is good possibility of growth in this sector for many stocks.

This sectors has provided good return on almost all the Steel Company in last one year.

Excellent return has been provided in past five years by Jindal Steel & Power Ltd.

"You're going to learn a million things, then you need to forget them all and focus on one." – Unknown

Tata Steel Long Product has also provided good return in last 1 year.

Long Term and Short Term Strategy investment is suggested for this sector with leading stocks with some short term targets too.

Power - Generation & Distribution

Historically, Indian power sector remembered for power-cuts, business losses, economic losses, system inefficiencies and many others. But now this sector has changed and progressing at a fast pace leading to happiness and prosperity everywhere in the country.

Power Sector in India is very much diversified. Our Sources of power generation range from conventional sources like coal, lignite, natural gas, oil, hydro nuclear power to viable non-conventional sources such as wind, solar, and agricultural and domestic waste. Electricity demand in the country has increased rapidly and is expected to rise further in the years to come. In order to meet the increasing demand for electricity in the country, massive addition to the installed generating capacity is required and the effort is on. Also sustained economic growth continues to drive electricity demand in India.

The Government of India's focus on attaining 'Power for all' has accelerated capacity addition in the country.

"To obtain financial freedom, one must be either a business owner, an investor, or both, generating passive income, particularly on a monthly basis." – Robert Kiyosaki

Things to Know Before Investing

Listed here are few of the companies of this sector which can be studied and analyzed by the readers for investment and building their portfolio. Some high level detail of the sector and stocks is described below.

S.No.	Company Name	Piotroski Score	Sales (In Cr) Year 2020
1	NTPC	6	109464
2	Power Grid Corporation of India	7	37743
3	Tata Power	4	29136
4	Adani Power	4	24467
5	Torrent Power	8	13640
6	Adani Transmission	8	11415
7	CESC Ltd	9	11014
8	NHPC	7	10008

Companies fall Mostly Under in Large Cap categories in Power – Generation and distribution Sector.

All Companies listed above have recorded 3 Year CAGR Positive Revenue and 3 Year CAGR Positive Net Profit indicating growing and profitable sector.

NTPC being at the Top on Turnover whereas Power Grid has the highest Market Capitalization.

Companies with High market Cap are PFC, NTPC, Adani Transmission, Tata Power, NHPC

"If you do not find a way to make money while you sleep, you will work until you die." – Warren Buffet

Ratio Beta is less than 1 for most of the companies in the sector indicating low volatility sector and hence long term investment can be targeted in this sector. PE Ratio is mix where many are above and many are below the Sector PE indicating there is good scope of growth in this sector for many stocks.

This sector has provided average return on Investment on almost all the Power Distribution and Generation sector Companies in last 1 to 5 years except for Adani Transmission.

Adani Transmission has provided fantastic return on investment in 5 years.

JSW Energy Limited, Tata Power Co Ltd, Torrent Power Limited have provided good short term returns with planned and timely entry and exit.

Long Term and Short Term Strategy investment is suggested for this sector with leading stocks.

Construction & Engineering

India's construction and engineering sector has witnessed a remarkable growth over the last few decades. This sector creates investment opportunities across various related sectors, like manufacturing, Steel, infrastructure etc.

This sector accounts for major investments (approx. – 40 %) of the total development investment. Around 16 per cent of the nation's working population depends on construction sector

"The best time, to plant a tree was 20 years ago. The second best time is today." – Ancient Chinese Proverb

Things to Know Before Investing

for its livelihood. The Indian construction industry employs over 30 million people and creates huge assets.

India, on its quest to become a global superpower, has made significant stride towards developing its construction and engineering sector. Connected technologies and an increase in associated investments will help firms realize new operational efficiencies.

Listed here are few of the companies of this sector which can be studied and analyzed by the readers for investment and building their portfolio. Some high level detail of the sector and stocks is described below.

S.No.	Company Name	Piotroski Score	Sales (In Cr) Year 2020
1	Larsen & Tubro Ltd	3	145452
2	NBCC	6	8087
3	PNC Infratech Ltd	7	5602
4	Ircon International Ltd.	7	5202
5	Ashoka Buildcon	7	5070
6	Sadbhav Engineering Ltd	7	3487
7	J Kumar Infraprojects Ltd.	7	2970
8	KNR Construction Ltd	5	2451
9	NCC Ltd	5	2451
10	HG Infra Engineering Ltd	5	2217
11	ITD Cementation India Ltd	5	2142
12	Capacite Infraprojects Ltd	5	1528

"There are certain things that cannot be adequately explained to a virgin either by words or pictures." – Alice Schroeder

Most Companies fall under Mid Cap categories except Larsen & Tubro Ltd

Most of Companies (except Sadbhav Engineering Ltd.) have registered 3 Year CAGR Positive Revenue. 3 Year CAGR Positive Net Profit is registered by all above except NBCC, Ashoka Buildcon and ITD Cementation India Ltd.

Larsen & Tubro Ltd being at the Top on Sales and has the highest market capitalization.

Ratio Beta is less than 1 for most of the companies indicating low volatility sector and hence long term investment can be targeted in this sector. PE Ratio is mix where many are above and many are below the Sector PE indicating there is good possibility of growth in this sector for many stocks.

Good return on Investment is recorded on PNC Infrratech Ltd, KNR Construction Ltd, NCC Ltd in past 2 years and by Ircon in past 5 years. NBCC has provided good short term returns with planned and timely entry and exit. Long Term and Short Term Strategy investment is suggested for this sector with leading stocks.

Auto Ancillaries

The Auto Ancillary Sector includes companies that provide parts and supporting equipment to the primary products of a vehicle company. This support may be in the form of Parts and components, Brakes, Suspension, etc.

"Games are won by players who focus on the playing field – not by those whose eyes are glued to the scoreboard." – Warren Buffett

The Auto Ancillary sector from India is mainly focused domestically. But gives the idea on the scale of opportunity and growth of this sectors looking at the data of last few years. An Auto Ancillary Industry is heavily dependent on the Automobile Industry.

This sector enable Automobile companies to focus on their core competencies while they are able to produce quality parts they specialize in. The high growth prospects of the Auto Ancillary Industry makes it one of the promising sector and Industry in the Indian markets.

Listed here are few of the companies of this sector which can be studied and analyzed by the readers for investment and building their portfolio. Some high level detail of the sector and stocks is described below.

S.No.	Company Name	Piotroski Score	Sales (In Cr) Year 2020
1	Motherson Sumi	5	63536
2	Sundaram Clayton Ltd	4	19858
3	Exide Industries	6	14471
4	Endurance Tech.	7	6917
5	Amara Raja Batteries	6	6839
6	Minda Industries	3	5465
7	Sundaram Fasten.	6	3723
8	Subros Ltd	6	1992
9	Suprajit Engineering	6	1562

"Do you know the only thing that gives me pleasure? It's to see my dividends coming in." – John D. Rockefeller

| 10 | JTEKT India Ltd | 7 | 1510 |
| 11 | Jamna Auto Industries | 3 | 1129 |

This sectors has small, mid and large market cap companies and most of them are performing and providing good return on investment.

Most of Companies are having 3 Year CAGR Positive Revenue indicating growing sector.

Endurance Tech., Amara Raja Batteries, Minda Industries, Sundaram Clayton, JTEKT India Ltd and Subros Ltd have registered 3 Year CAGR Positive Net Profit. Others have registered negative 3 year CAGR Net Profit indicating very high competition in the sector among peer companies.

Motherson Sumi is at the Top on Sales and Market Capitalization

Ratio Beta is less than 1 for most of the companies indicating low volatility sector and hence long term investment can be targeted in this sector. PE Ratio is high for most of the companies as compared to Sector PE indicating prices are overrated but investors are ready to pay the Current Market Price.

Good return is received on Investment on stocks of Motherson Sumi, Endurance Tech., Amara Raja Battery., Sundaram Fastenter, Suprajit Engineering, Jamna Auto Industries, Minda Industries, Sundaram Clayton Ltd.

"The best chance to deploy capital is when things are going down."
– Warren Buffett

Banking

The Indian Banking industry has historically been one of the most stable systems globally. Despite global upheavals our banking system has remained stable and tough sustaining all pressure.

The Indian banking system consists of public sector banks, private sector banks, foreign banks, regional rural banks, urban cooperative banks and rural cooperative banks.

The largest and the oldest bank which is still in existence is the State Bank of India **(SBI).**

Investment-driven growth require access to low cost capital, and this what banking sector is providing and helping to boost the economy.

The digital payments revolution will trigger massive changes in the way credit is disbursed. Payments on Unified Payments Interface (UPI) has picked up well and is growing. NPAs (Non-Performing Assets) of commercial banks has done huge recovery in FY19, which has further supported the banking sector to perform well.

The government has consistently strived to promote financial inclusion through various initiatives targeted to bring the country's under banked population under the banking gamut.

Listed here are few of the companies of this sector which can be studied and analyzed by the readers for investment and

"Much success can be attributed to inactivity. Most investors cannot resist the temptation to constantly buy and sell." – Warren Buffett

building their portfolio. Some high level detail of the sector and stocks is described below.

S.No.	Company Name	Piotroski Score	Sales (In Cr) Year 2020
1	SBI	6	269851
2	HDFC Bank	2	122189
3	ICICI Bank	6	84835
4	BOB	7	78894
5	Axis Bank	5	63715
6	Kotak Mahindra Bank	5	33474
7	Indusind Bank	5	28782
8	AU Small Finance Bank	3	3000

This sectors has large market cap companies which are mostly performing and providing good return on investment on long term basis.

HDFC has the highest Market capitalization whereas SBI has the highest Turnover.

Ratio Beta is more than 1 for most of the companies indicating high volatility sector and hence short term profit booking can also be targeted in this sector along with long terms investment. PE of most of the stocks are less than sector PE indicating there is good possibility of growth in this sector.

Good return on Investment is observed on most of the banks mentioned above in Short and Long Term.

"I have probably purchased fifty 'hot tips' in my career, maybe even more. When I put them all together, I know I am a net loser."
– Charles Schwab

FMCG

The Fast-moving consumer goods (FMCG) sector is the 4th largest sector of the Indian economy. FMCG goods are produced, distributed, marketed and consumed within a short span of time. If we see from the consumer perspective, these products are purchased frequently, have low cost, short shelf life and consumed fast. From the market perspective, these are high volume, low margin, and high turnover products.

FMCG products that dominate today are beverages, detergents, toiletries, candies, dry goods, over the counter drugs, tooth cleaning products, cosmetics, chocolates etc. Since the sector encompasses a diverse range of products, different companies dominate the market in various sub-sectors. However, some of the top FMCG companies in India are ITC, Hindustan Unilever, Dabur, Godrej Consumer, Marico, Colgate and others.

The FMCG industry in India can be divided into the demographics of rural and urban India. While the urban market contributes 60% of the consumption revenue of the FMCG, the semi-urban and rural segments are growing at a rate that cannot be ignored.

Listed here are few of the companies of this sector which can be studied and analyzed by the readers for investment and building their portfolio. Some high level detail of the sector and stocks is described below.

"Don't judge each day by the harvest you reap but by the seeds that you plant." – Robert Louis Stevenson

S.No.	Company Name	Piotroski Score	Sales (In Cr) Year 2020
1	ITC	5	49404
2	Hindustan Unilever	5	39783
3	Nestle India	7	12368
4	Britannia Industries	4	11599
5	Godrej Consumer	5	9910
6	Dabur India	4	8684
7	Marico	6	7315
8	P & G Hygiene	7	3001
9	Emami Ltd	9	2654

This sector has mostly Large and Mid-Cap companies.

Companies with Highest Market Cap is Hindustan Unilever whereas ITC has highest turnover.

All companies listed have registered 3 Year CAGR Positive Revenue and Net Profit (Except for Emami Ltd).

Few companies in this sectors have provided good return on investment in short and long term in last 5 years.

Ratio - Beta of almost all companies mentioned is less than 1 indicating less risk and volatility and safe for investment but may generate low return. PE Ratio is high for most of the companies as compared to Sector PE indicating prices are overrated.

"A winning strategy must include losing." – Rich Dad :-)

Cement

India's cement industry is the second largest in the world, in terms of production of the global installed capacity and it is generating employment for over 1 million people.

With per capita cement consumption at less than 200 kg when the world boasts of an average of 500 kg., we see rapid growth of this sector in near future.

Indian cement industry consists the mix of regional and national players. Cement being a bulk commodity is freight-intensive and transporting it over long distances proves uneconomical and hence there are many regional players in this sector. Although there has been lot of consolidation in the past, the trend is likely to continue, and we may be witnessing more acquisitions in coming few years.

With initiatives such as 'Housing for All' and major infrastructure projects with respect to Rail, Road by Govt. of India will boost the growth of the cement industry significantly.

The industry believes that there would be a surge in demand due to the planning and execution on the projects by Govt. of India through infrastructure and housing projects. This will lead to increase of per capita cement consumption in the country significantly in the coming 10 years.

It is expected that Cement Industry will have to further go for capacity expansion to meet the future demand.

"Wall Street Makes Money on Activity and you make Money on Inactivity." – Warren Buffett

The future looks very optimistic and promising for cement sector, looking into the potential for development in the infrastructure, housing and construction sector. A significant factor which aids the growth of this sector is the high availability of raw materials for making cement, such as limestone and coal.

Listed here are few of the companies of this sector which can be studied and analyzed by the readers for investment and building their portfolio. Some high level detail of the sector and stocks is described below.

S.No.	Company Name	Piotroski Score	Sales (In Cr) Year 2020
1	Ultra Tech	6	42124
2	Ambuja Cements	6	27103
3	ACC	6	15657
4	Shree Cement	8	12868
5	Prism Johnson Ltd	5	5956
6	J K cement	7	5801
7	Ramco Cement	4	5389
8	Heidelberg Cement	7	2169
9	Shree Digvijay Cement	8	469

All companies mentioned above have registered 3 Year CAGR Positive Revenue and 3 Year CAGR Positive Net Profit (except Ramco Cement) indicating growing and performing sector.

"The individual investor should act consistently as an investor and not as a speculator." – Ben Graham

Ultra Tech being at the Top on Market Capitalization and Sales is Cement Sector. Companies with High market Cap are Ambuja Cements, Ultra Tech, Shree Cement, ACC, Ramco Cement and J K cement.

Ratio – Beta of almost all companies mentioned is less than 1 indicating less risk and volatility and safe for investment but may generate low return. PE Ratio is mix where many are above and many are below the Sector PE indicating there is good possibility of growth in this sector for many stocks.

Good return is recorded on Ultra Tech, Shree Cement, Ramco Cement and Prism in las2 years.

Excellent Return on J K cement is recorded in short and long term.

Long Term and Short Term Strategy investment is suggested for this sector with leading stocks.

Automotive

India's automobile sector is emerging out from the adverse impact of COVID-19 and continuing on its path to becoming the third-largest automobile market in the world. India is expected to displace Japan as the third largest auto market.

In four wheeler segment, Mini cars and hatchback cars have been the mainstay for the automobile industry in India, with share around 50 percent. These segments will continue to

"Stop trying to predict the direction of the stock market, the economy or the elections." – Warren Buffett

maintain a dominant position, but the majority of growth is expected to come from new segments such as compact SUVs, sedans, and luxury vehicles.

The two wheeler segment dominates the Indian market in terms of volume owing to its growing middle class and a young population. Moreover, the growing interest of the companies in exploring the rural markets further added to the growth of the sector.

The growth drivers in the automotive industry has remained intact and the sector is likely to see an increased upward trend in demand in the coming years. The Government's 'Make in India' initiative has played an important role in elevating the country's position for ease of doing business in the last three to four years. Today, India is looked upon as a favorable destination for low-cost manufacturing.

India is also a prominent auto exporter and has strong export growth expectations for the near future. In addition, several initiatives by the Government of India and major automobile players in the Indian market are expected to make India a leader in the two-wheeler and four-wheeler market.

The automobile industry is also supported by various factors such as availability of skilled labour at low cost, robust R&D centers, and low-cost steel production.

Indian automotive industry (including component manufacturing) is expected to reach Rs. 16–18 trillion by 2026.

> *"You get recession, you get stock market declines. If you don't understand that's going to happen, then you are not ready and you will not do well in the markets." – Peter Lynch*

Things to Know Before Investing

Listed here are few of the companies of this sector which can be studied and analyzed by the readers for investment and building their portfolio. Some high level detail of the sector and stocks is described below.

S.No.	Company Name	Piotroski Score	Sales (In Cr) Year 2020
1	Tata Motors	2	261067
2	Mahindra and Mahindra	3	95179
3	Maruti Suzuki India Ltd.	4	75660
4	Bajaj Auto	8	29918
5	Hero Motocorp	6	29253
6	TVS Motor Co.	3	18849
7	Ashok Leyland	4	17647
8	Eicher Motors	4	9153

All Companies listed above fall under Large Cap categories.

All Companies listed above have recorded 3 Year CAGR Positive Revenue except Tata Motors and Ashok Leyland. 3 Year CAGR Positive Net Profit is recorded by Tata Motors, Bajaj Auto, Eicher Motor, Hero Motocorp and TVS Motor Co.

Few Companies like Maruti, M&M and Ashok Leyland have registered negative 3 Year CAGR Net Profit indicating high cost pressure and increasing operation efficiency needed.

"Get inside information from the president and you will lose half of your money. If you get it from the chairman of the board, you will lose all your money." – Jim Rogers

Maruti Suzuki holds Top slot on Sales and Market Capitalization.

Ratio Beta is more than 1 for few and less than 1 for others indicating few stocks to be more volatile.

In last one year, most of the stocks given good returns and TATA Motors has given excellent returns on the investment.

Long Term and Short Term Strategy investment is suggested for this sector with leading stocks.

Chemical

India's chemical industry is extremely diversified and can be broadly classified into bulk chemicals, specialty chemicals, agrochemicals, petrochemicals, polymers and fertilizers.

Covering more than 80,000 commercial products, India accounts for around 16% of the world production of dyestuffs and dye intermediates. Indian colorants industry has emerged a key player with a global market share of around 15%.

India's proximity to the world's source of petrochemicals feedstock, enables it to benefit on economies of scale.

The demand for chemicals is expected to expand by 7–9% per annum by 2025.

Listed here are few of the companies of this sector which can be studied and analyzed by the readers for investment and

Courage taught me no matter how bad a crisis gets ... any sound investment will eventually pay off." – Carlos Slim Helu

building their portfolio. Some high level detail of the sector and stocks is described below.

S.No.	Company Name	Piotroski Score	Sales (In Cr) Year 2020
1	Aarti Inds.	7	4186
2	Atul	6	4093
3	GHCL	6	3305
4	Solar Industries.	4	2237
5	Vinati Organics	7	1028
6	Gulshan Polyols Ltd	8	620
7	Advanced Enzyme.	6	443

This sectors has small, mid and large market cap companies and many are good performing and providing good return on investment.

All above companies have recorded 3 Year CAGR Positive Revenue and 3 Year CAGR Positive Net Profit except Gulshan Polyols Ltd.

Aarti Industries holds Top Slot on Market Capitalization and Sales.

Companies with High market Cap Aarti Industries, Atul and Vinati Organics.

Beta of most of all high turnover companies is less than 1 indicating less risk and volatility. PE of most of the stocks are higher to industry PE.

"Everyone has the brainpower to follow the stock market. If you made it through fifth-grade math, you can do it." – Peter Lynch

Excellent return is received last 2 years on Advanced Enzyme and on Atul, Vinati, and Aarti in last 5 years.

Long Term investment is suggested with leading stocks and short term investment with few stocks.

Breweries & Distilleries

India has over 30% of the population consuming alcohol which are mostly led by the UTs and southern States, the industry boasts of being the third largest and fastest growing market for alcoholic beverages.

The country is not only the largest market for the spirit, it is also the largest global producer of whisky. India consumes 48% of the world's whisky. It is the fastest-growing market and the largest producer of the spirit.

Per capita consumption, at 4 litres of beer a year, is a fraction of that in the west and many other emerging Asian economies, suggesting there is plenty of room to grow.

Listed here are few of the companies of this sector which can be studied and analyzed by the readers for investment and building their portfolio. Some high level detail of the sector and stocks is described below.

> *"Business and financial intelligence are not picked up within the four walls of school. You pick them up on the streets. In school, you are taught how to manage other people's money. On the streets, you are taught how to make money." – Ajaero Tony Martins*

Things to Know Before Investing

S.No.	Company Name	Piotroski Score	Sales (In Cr) Year 2020
1	United Spirits Ltd	6	9325
2	United Breweries	6	6504
3	Radico Khaitan Ltd	7	2427
4	Globus Spirits	8	1168
5	IFB Agro	7	985
6	Associated Alcohols & Breweries	9	522
7	GM Breweries	6	468

This sectors has small, mid and large market cap companies.

Companies mentioned above have recorded 3 Year CAGR Positive Revenue and 3 Year CAGR Positive Net Profit indicating healthy growth of the most of the above companies in the sector.

United Spirits Ltd has the highest Market Capitalization and Sales.

Beta of all companies is less than 1 indicating less risk and volatility. PE Ratio is mix where many are above and many are below the Sector PE indicating there is good possibility of growth in this sector for many stocks.

Globus Spirits has provided good return on investment in past 2 years.

"In many ways, the stock market is like the weather in that if you don't like the current conditions all you have to do is wait a while."
– Low Simpson

Cables

The wire and cable market in India, which comprises nearly 40 per cent of the electrical industry, is growing at a CAGR of 15 per cent.

Electricity demand is forecast to nearly double in coming 10 years. This has generated need of quality electrical infrastructure supporting its growth for several years to come and it augurs well for the development of wires and cables industry in India. Being one of the key segments of power sector, wires and cables sector is experiencing an escalating demand owing to the growth in power generation infrastructure.

Listed here are few of the companies of this sector which can be studied and analyzed by the readers for investment and building their portfolio. Some high level detail of the sector and stocks is described below.

S.No.	Company Name	Piotroski Score	Sales (In Cr) Year 2020
1	Polycab	7	8829
2	Sterlite Technologies	5	5154
3	KEI Ind	5	4887
4	Finolex Cables Ltd	5	2877
5	Vindhya Telelink Ltd	3	1883
6	Universal Cables	4	1568
7	Birla Cables	5	223

"The entrance strategy is actually more important than the exit strategy." – Edward Lampert

This sectors has Small, Mid-Market cap companies and is a growing sector.

All companies have registered 3 Year CAGR Positive Revenue and Year CAGR Positive Net Profit except Birla Cables.

POLYCAB being at the Top on Market Capitalisation and Sales.

Ratio Beta is more than 1 for few and less than 1 for others indicating few stocks to be more volatile. PE Ratio is mix where many are above and many are below the Sector PE indicating there is good possibility of growth in this sector for many stocks

Excellent return is recorded in POLYCAB in last 2 years and in KEI industries and Sterlite technologies in last 5 years.

Long Term and Short Term Strategy investment is suggested for this sector with leading stocks.

Housing Finance

Housing Finance Companies have grown fast in last 5 years and high demand in affordable housing segment is further going to boost the growth in coming 10 years.

Housing is a primary necessity and is a basic indicator of growth and social well-being. Development of housing is also an accelerator that has impact on other sectors like Steel, construction and infrastructure sector, cable, power, road and highways as it generates demand for supporting

"You need to know very well when to move away, or give up the loss, and not allow the anxiety to trick you into trying again."
– Warren Buffett

industries and leads to creation of job opportunities. Development of housing in a country is a sign of economic welfare and prosperity. Hence Housing Finance Sectors plays a key role in growth of this sector and other integrated supporting sectors

Listed here are few of the companies of this sector which can be studied and analyzed by the readers for investment and building their portfolio. Some high level detail of the sector and stocks is described below.

S.No.	Company Name	Piotroski Score	Sales (In Cr) Year 2020
1	HDFC	3	101725
2	LIC Housing Finance	5	19736
3	Indiabulls Housing Finance Ltd	4	11399
4	PNB Housing Finance	6	8481
5	Sundaram Finance	5	4695
6	IIFL Finance Ltd	4	2608
7	GIC Housing Finance Ltd	4	1247

This sectors has small, mid and large market cap companies.

All companies mentioned above (except Sundaram Finance) have recorded 3 Year CAGR Positive Revenue and all companies (except Indiabulls Housing Finance and GIC Housing Finance) have registered 3 Year CAGR Positive Net Profit.

The question should not be how much I will profit on this trade! The true question is; will I be fine if I don't profit from this trade."
– Yvan Byeajee

HDFC has highest Market Capitalization and Sales.

Excellent return on investment received on IIFL Finance and Sundaram Finance in last 1 year and HDFC and IIFL Finance in last 5 years.

Oil & Gas Marketing and Distribution

The Oil/Gas Distribution Industry comprises companies that move two of the most important energy commodities, and their derivatives, from the wellhead to the ultimate consumer.

In Oil and Gas business, the marketing and distribution of petroleum products takes place on a very large and global scale. Every day, hundreds of millions of companies, distributors and individuals buy these products at wholesale or directly from retail outlets.

Marketing and distribution of petroleum products is a complex and wide-ranging sector of the international petroleum industry.

Listed here are few of the companies of this sector which can be studied and analyzed by the readers for investment and building their portfolio. Some high level detail of the sector and stocks is described below.

S.No.	Company Name	Piotroski Score	Sales (In Cr) Year 2020
1	IOCL	2	484362
2	GAIL	5	72508

"It's OK to be wrong; it's unforgivable to stay wrong." – Martin Zweig

3	Petronet LNG	7	35452
4	Indraprastha Gas	7	6485
5	Castrol India	6	2996
6	Mahanagar Gas	8	2972
7	Gulf Oil Lubric.	5	1643

This sectors has mostly large market cap companies.

All companies (except Castrol India) listed above have recorded 3 Year CAGR Positive Revenue and all companies (except Castrol India and IOCL) have registered 3 Year CAGR Positive Net Profit.

IOCL has highest Market Capitalization and Sales.

Beta of all companies is less than 1 indicating less risk and volatility in this sector and good for long term investment. PE Ratio is mix where many are above and many are below the Sector PE indicating there is good possibility of growth in this sector for many stocks

Indraprastra Gas Limited has provided comparatively good return in last 2 years.

Most companies in this sector has provided very average return in last 5 years on investment.

> *"Dramatic and emotional trading experiences tend to be negative. Pride is a great banana peel, as are hope, fear, and greed. My biggest slip-ups occurred shortly after I got emotionally involved with positions." – Ed Seykota*

Realty

After three years of business disruptions caused by demonetization, implementation of GST and the realty law RERA, and the NBFC crisis, the market had started stabilizing and Year 2020 was expected to bring some good news to all in Realty Sector.

But all hopes subsided when COVID-19 global pandemic hit India, forcing the government to impose a national lockdown from end week of March 2020.

Instead of recovery and growth, 2020 brought more pain and distress in the realty sector.

Housing sales began to improve only from October 2020 onwards.

The softening of interest rates on home loans to around 7% and rock bottom housing prices coupled with attractive special offers from cash-starved developers were positive factors that paved buyers' return to the market, albeit at a slower pace from Oct 2020.

Revival of Realty Sectors can gear up in 2021, provided the government extends a helping hand and injects enough stimulus to boost the sector and the overall economy. But the positive side is that all sectors have started to gear up after pandemic and it will have positive impact of realty sector also.

"Risk no more that you can afford to lose, and also risk enough so that a win is meaningful." – Ed Seykota

Listed here are few of the companies of this sector which can be studied and analyzed by the readers for investment and building their portfolio. Some high level detail of the sector and stocks is described below.

S.No.	Company Name	Piotroski Score	Sales (In Cr) Year 2020
1	India Bulls Real Estate	4	3270
2	Brigade Enterprises	3	2632
3	Godrej Prop	3	2441
4	Oberoi Realty	4	2237
5	Purvankara	7	2128
6	Ahluwalia Contracts (India)	5	1884
7	Kolte Patil Dev	5	1129

This sectors has mainly Mid and Large market cap companies.

All companies listed above have recorded 3 Year CAGR Positive Revenue and Godrej Properties, Oberoi Realty, Kolte Patil Dev have registered 3 Year CAGR Positive Net Profit.

Godrej properties has the highest Market Capitalisation and India Bulls Real Estate having highest sales.

Ratio Beta is more than 1 for few and less than 1 for others indicating few stocks to be more volatile and may be planned for investment for short term return. PE Ratio is mix where

"Dramatic and emotional trading experiences tend to be negative. Pride is a great banana peel, as are hope, fear, and greed. My biggest slip-ups occurred shortly after I got emotionally involved with positions." – Ed Seykota

many are above and many are below the Sector PE indicating there is good possibility of growth in this sector for many stocks.

Excellent return is provided by Godrej properties and Brigade Enterprises in 2 years and 5 years in this sector.

Transport and Logistics

Efficient transportation and movement of goods is the backbone of any country's growth, and is has a multiplier effect on the growth of the economy. India's transport and logistics sector has played a key role in essential and emergency passenger transport and supply of essential goods and drugs across the country amidst the COVID-19 related lockdown.

Investment and technological adoption in transportation and logistics infrastructure would lead to higher convenience, affordability, and better urban space design for pedestrians and vehicles.

Also growing Ecommerce platform is boosting this sector to a great extent.

Listed here are few of the companies of this sector which can be studied and analyzed by the readers for investment and building their portfolio. Some high level detail of the sector and stocks is described below.

"The key to long-term survival and prosperity has a lot to do with the money management techniques incorporated into the technical system." – Ed Seykota

S.No.	Company Name	Piotroski Score	Sales (In Cr) Year 2020
1	Aegis Logistics	7	7183
2	Container Corp	7	6473
3	Mahindra Logistics Ltd	4	3471
4	Blue Dart Exp.	3	3175
5	VRL Logistics	5	2118
6	Gati	5	1711
7	TCI Express	6	1031

This sectors has small, mid and large market cap companies.

All companies mentioned above have registered 3 Year CAGR Positive Revenue all companies (Blue Dart Exp. and Container Corp) have registered 3 Year CAGR Positive Net Profit.

Container Corporation being at the Top on Market Capitalization whereas AEGIS Logistics has highest sales.

Beta of all companies is less than 1 indicating less risk and volatility. PE Ratio is mix where many are above and many are below the Sector PE indicating there is good possibility of growth in this sector for many stocks

Blue dart Express has given good return in last 2 years and AEGIS logistics in last 5 years.

Tire and Rubber

The Rubber Industry is a key sector in the Indian economy with a turnover of around 12,000 Crs per annum. India is the

"The markets are the same now as they were five or ten years ago because they keep changing-just like they did then." – Ed Seykota

largest producer and third largest consumer of natural rubber in the world. But still India is a natural rubber deficit country where we have to import natural rubber to meet the demand of this sector. Around 30 to 40% of the requirement of natural rubber is to be imported as there is difference between production and consumption. Import is mostly done from Indonesia, Malaysia, Vietnam and Thailand.

Tyre consumes around 70% of the rubber whereas the rest is consumed by tubes, footwear, rubber bands and other industries. While the Tyre industry is largely dominated by the organized sector, the unorganized sector is predominant with respect to bicycle tires.

The Indian Tyre industry is expected to show a healthy growth rate of 9–10% over the next five years. Since the Automotive industry is slated to grow, Rubber and Tyre Sector is also expected to grow.

Listed here are few of the companies of this sector which can be studied and analyzed by the readers for Investment and building their portfolio. Some high level detail of the sector and stocks is described below.

S.No.	Company Name	Piotroski Score	Sales (In Cr) Year 2020
1	Apollo Tyre	4	16327
2	MRF	8	16239

"Markets are fundamentally volatile. No way around it. Your problem is not in the math. There is no math to get you out of having to experience uncertainty." – Ed Seykota

3	J K Tyre	5	8724
4	CEAT	5	6778
5	Balkrishna Industries	7	4811
6	Goodyear India Ltd	6	1745

This sectors has small, mid and large market cap companies

All companies listed above have recorded 3 Year CAGR Positive Revenue and Balkrishna Ind, has registered 3 Year CAGR Positive Net Profit.

Balkrishna Industries has the highest market capitalization and Apollo is highest in Sales.

Ratio Beta is more than 1 for few and less than 1 for others indicating few stocks to be more volatile. PE Ratio is mix where many are above and many are below the Sector PE indicating there is good possibility of growth in this sector for many stocks.

Balkrishna Industries, CEAT Apollo and JK tires has provided good return in last 2 years and Balkrishna Industries in last 5 years also.

Long Term and Short Term Strategy investment is suggested for this sector with leading stocks.

Agro Chemicals

India agrochemical market is expected to grow at a fast pace in the coming 5 years. Increasing population, decreasing per

"Trading is a waiting game. You sit, you wait, and you make a lot of money all at once. Profits come in bunches. The trick when going sideways between home runs is not to lose too much in between." – Michael Covel

capita availability of land & focus on increasing agricultural yield are major factors driving India's agrochemical market. Also growing demand for food grain, need for high land productivity, new policies are launched to encourage maximum production of fertilizers are major growth factors of India agrochemical market.

The Indian agriculture sector is currently facing critical challenges like reduction in agricultural land, decreasing farm size, increasing pest attacks and low per hectare yield position which is being positively impacting on India's agrochemical market.

Listed here are few of the companies of this sector which can be studied and analyzed by the readers for investment and building their portfolio. Some high level detail of the sector and stocks is described below.

S.No.	Company Name	Piotroski Score	Sales (In Cr) Year 2020
1	UPL	9	35755
2	Bayer Crop Science Ltd.	8	3609
3	PI Industries	4	3366
4	Rallis India	8	2251
5	Sharda Cropchem	6	2003
6	Dhanuka Agritech	7	1122

"When a market makes a historic high, it is telling you something. No matter how many people tell you why the market shouldn't be that high, or why nothing has changed, the mere fact that the price is at a new high tells you something has changed." – Larry Hite

This sectors has mid and large market cap companies which are all performing and providing good return on investment.

All companies have recorded 3 Year CAGR Positive Revenue and Many companies with 3 Year CAGR Positive Net Profit.

UPL being at the Top on Market Capitalization and Sales.

Companies with High market Cap are UPL, PI industries and BAYER crop Science Limited.

Beta of most of all high turnover companies is less than 1 indicating less risk and volatility. PE of most of the stocks are less than sector PE indicating there is good possibility of growth in this sector.

Dhanuka Agritech and Sharda Cropchem have provided good returns in last 2 years and PI industries in last 5 years.

Food Processing

In India, Food Processing sector has emerged as a high-growth and high-profit sector due to its immense potential for value addition, particularly within the food processing industry. The Government of India has been instrumental and making all efforts for the growth and development of the food processing industry.

The Indian food processing industry is poised for huge growth.

Listed here are few of the companies of this sector which can be studied and analyzed by the readers for investment and

"Throughout my trading career, I have continually witnessed examples of other people that I have known being ruined by a failure to respect risk. If you don't take a hard look at risk," it will take you. – Larry Hite

building their portfolio. Some high level detail of the sector and stocks is described below.

S.No.	Company Name	Piotroski Score	Sales (In Cr) Year 2020
1	KRBL	9	4499
2	Zydus Wellness	7	1766
3	Heritage Foods	3	2725
4	Jubilant Foodworks	5	3927
5	Varun Beverages Ltd	7	7129
6	GRM Overseas Ltd	6	766

This sectors has small, mid and large market cap companies.

All companies listed above have recorded 3 Year CAGR Positive Revenue and all companies (Except Heritage foods) have reported 3 Year CAGR Positive Net Profit also.

Jubilant Foodworks is at the Top on Market Capitalization and Varun Beverages has the highest Sales.

Beta of all companies is less than 1 indicating less risk and volatility. PE Ratio is mix where many are above and many are below the Sector PE indicating there is good possibility of growth in this sector for many stocks.

Zydus wellness, Jubilant Foodworks, Varun Beverages and GRM overseas limited have provided good returns in last 2 years and 5 years.

"We approach markets backwards. The first thing we ask is not what can we make, but how much can we lose. We play a defensive game."
– Larry Hite

Hospital and Medical Services

This sector is facing an acute crisis in terms of a shortage of relevant healthcare infrastructure, especially in rural and sub-urban areas. It includes hospitals, medical devices, health insurance, telemedicine, clinical trials, medical tourism, and medical equipment. Growing cases of lifestyle diseases, the demand for affordable healthcare, technological advancements, and penetration of health insurance are some of the key growth drivers for this sector.

The availability of bed and doctor per 1000 people is abysmally low and there is huge scope of impermanent possible in this sector.

Listed here are few of the companies of this sector which can be studied and analyzed by the readers for investment and building their portfolio. Some high level detail of the sector and stocks is described below.

S.No.	Company Name	Piotroski Score	Sales (In Cr) Year 2020
1	Apollo Hospital Enterprises	6	11246
2	Dr Lal Path labs	5	1330
3	Max Healthcare Institute Ltd	1	1134
4	Metropolis Healthcare Ltd	4	856
5	Poly Medicure Ltd	6	687
6	Thyrocare Tech.	5	433

"If you diversify, control your risk, and go with the trend, it just has to work." – Larry Hite

This sectors has mid and large market cap companies.

All companies listed above have recorded 3 Year CAGR Positive Revenue and 3 Year CAGR Positive Net Profit indicating healthy growth of the sector and companies.

Apollo Hospital Enterprises holds Top position on Market Capitalization and Sales. Companies with High market capitalization are Dr. Lal Path Lab, Metropolis healthcare, Max healthcare institute.

Beta of all companies is less than 1 indicating less risk and volatility. PE Ratio is mix where many are above and many are below the Sector PE indicating there is good possibility of growth in this sector for many stocks.

Dr. Lal Pathlabs, Thyrocare, Poly Medicure limited, Metropolis Healthcare, Apollo and Max healthcare limited have given good returns in last 2 years and Poly Medicure has given good returns in last 5 years.

Hotel

Hotel industry in India has grown significantly in the past and is expected to grow fast in the coming 5 years. In the past few years, the occupancy rate the major hotels has increased at least two folds. The hotel industry is growing at about 7 per cent per annum and many experts believe that it may

"Never risk more than 1% of total account equity on any one trade. By risking 1%, I am indifferent to any individual trade. Keeping your risk small and constant is absolutely critical." – Larry Hite

fall short of meeting the long term demands of the thriving market.

Listed here are few of the companies of this sector which can be studied and analyzed by the readers for investment and building their portfolio. Some high level detail of the sector and stocks is described below.

S.No.	Company Name	Piotroski Score	Sales (In Cr) Year 2020
1	Indian Hotel	5	4463
2	Mahindra Holiday	2	2371
3	EIH Ltd	6	1596
4	Chalet Hotel	5	981
5	Lemon Tree Hotels Ltd	1	669
6	EIH Associated Hotel Ltd	5	249

This sectors has small, mid and large market cap companies

All companies (except EIH Associated) have recorded 3 Year CAGR Positive Revenue and Indian Hotel, EIH Ltd and Lemon Tree Hotel have registered 3 Year CAGR Positive Net Profit.

Indian Hotels being at the Top on Market Capitalization and Sales.

Beta of most of all high turnover companies is less than 1 indicating less risk and volatility.

Most of the Stocks in Hotel Sector have not provided good returns in the last 5 years.

"Win or lose, everybody gets what they want out of the market. Some people seem to like to lose, so they win by losing money." – Ed Seykota

Plantation – Tea

Currently, tea is produced in about 45 countries. But, a major chunk of the global tea output (approx. 85 %) comes from the Asian region with five countries, viz., China, India, Sri Lanka, Kenya and Indonesia.

This sector provides direct employment to 1.2 million people and supports to over three million dependents of tea garden workers. Women accounts for 50 per cent of the employment in the sector but the tea sector is confronted with several challenges which are threatening the long term viability of the industry. The sector is reeling under cost pressures due to price stagnation. There is increasing cost of production, mismatch between demand-supply, high transaction costs, challenges for fair price discovery at the auctions and climate change problem.

Listed here are few of the companies of this sector which can be studied and analyzed by the readers for investment and building their portfolio. Some high level detail of the sector and stocks is described below.

S.No.	Company Name	Piotroski Score	Sales (In Cr) Year 2020
1	Tata Consumer Products Ltd.	6	9637
2	Tata Coffee	8	1966
3	Mcleod Russel	4	1142

"Don't think about what the market's going to do; you have absolutely no control over that. Think about what you're going to do if it gets there." – William Eckhardt

4	CCL Products	6	1139
5	Jayahree Tea	4	717
6	Rossell India	5	309

This sectors has small, mid and large market cap companies.

Except Mcleod Russel and Jayshree Tea, all companies have recorded 3 Year CAGR Positive Revenue. All except Tata coffee have registered 3 Year CAGR Positive Net Profit.

TATA consumer products limited holds Top Slot for Market Capitalization and Sales.

Beta of all companies is less than 1 indicating less risk and volatility. PE Ratio is mix where many are above and many are below the Sector PE indicating there is good possibility of growth in this sector for many stocks

TATA consumer products limited, TATA coffee, ROSSELL India limited, Mcleod Russell have shown good returns in past 2 years TATA consumer products has shown good returns in last 5 years.

Consumer/Electronics

This sector is growing at a very fast pace and expected to double by 2025.

In addition to the urban market, there is a lot of scope for growth from the rural market with consumption expected to

"Traders focus almost entirely on where to enter a trade. In reality, the entry size is often more important than the entry price."
– Jack D. Schwager

grow in these areas as penetration of brands increases. Demand for durables like refrigerators and consumer electronic goods are likely to witness an increased demand in the coming years, especially in the rural areas as the rural electrification is progressing fast. Growing awareness, easier access, and changing lifestyle have been the key growth drivers for the consumer market.

Listed here are few of the companies of this sector which can be studied and analyzed by the readers for investment and building their portfolio. Some high level detail of the sector and stocks is described below.

S.No.	Company Name	Piotroski Score	Sales (In Cr) Year 2020
1	Bharat Electronics Ltd	6	12967
2	Voltas	3	7658
3	Whirlpool India	6	5992
4	Dixon Technology.	7	4400
5	Symphony	6	1102

This sectors has small, mid and large market cap companies.

All companies listed above have reported 3 Year CAGR Positive Revenue and 3 Year CAGR Positive Net Profit.

"Michael Jordan didn't become a great basketball player because he wanted to do product endorsements. Van Gogh didn't become a great painter because he dreamed that one day his paintings would sell for $50 million." – Jack D. Schwager

Bharat Electronics maintains (BEL) Top Slot on Market Capitalization and Sales.

Companies with High market Capitalization are Whirlpool India limited, DIXON Technologies, Voltas and BEL.

Beta of all companies is less than 1 indicating less risk and volatility in the sector. PE of most of the stocks are higher to industry PE indicating there is further possibility of growth in the sector

Fantastic return is provided by VOLTAS, DIXON and WHIRLPOOL in last 5 years and BEL in last 2 years

Mining & Mineral

The Mining industry in India is a major economic activity which contributes significantly to the growth of economy of India.

The GDP contribution of the mining industry varies from 2.2% to 2.5% only but going by the GDP of the total industrial sector it contributes around 8% to 11%.

Indian mining industry provides job opportunities to more than million people.

Listed here are few of the companies of this sector which can be studied and analyzed by the readers for investment and building their portfolio. Some high level detail of the sector and stocks is described below.

> *"Risk management is the most important thing to be well understood. Undertrade, undertrade, undertrade is my second piece of advice. Whatever you think your position ought to be, cut it at least in half."*
> *– Bruce Kovner*

Things to Know Before Investing

S.No.	Company Name	Piotroski Score	Sales (In Cr) Year 2020
1	Coal India	4	96080
2	Vedanta	4	84447
3	NMDC	5	11699
4	GMDC	3	1673
5	MOIL – Manganese Ore India Ltd	4	1038

This sectors has mid and large market cap companies.

All companies listed above have reported 3 Year CAGR Positive Revenue and Coal India and NMDC have reported 3 Year CAGR Positive Net Profit also.

COAL INDIA LIMITED has the highest Market Capitalization and Sales.

Companies with High market Cap COALINDIA LIMITED, NMDC and VEDANTA.

Beta of most of all high turnover companies is less than 1 indicating less risk and volatility in this sector. PE Ratio is mix where many are above and many are below the Sector PE indicating there is good possibility of growth in this sector for many stocks

VEDANTA has given good growth in last 2 years and 5 years

"Make sure you have an edge. Know what your edge is. And have rigid risk control rules." – Monroe Trout.

Plastic

The Indian plastics industry made significant progress and the sector has grown and diversified rapidly. The industry spans the country and hosts more than 2,000 exporters. It employs about 4 million people and comprises more than 30,000 processing units, 85–90% of which are small and medium-sized enterprises.

Listed here are few of the companies of this sector which can be studied and analyzed by the readers for investment and building their portfolio. Some high level detail of the sector and stocks is described below.

S.No.	Company Name	Piotroski Score	Sales (In Cr) Year 2020
1	Supreme Industries	6	5511
2	Finolex Ind	7	2985
3	Astral Poly Technik Ltd	8	2577
4	Nilkamal Ltd	7	2257

This sectors has mid and large market cap companies.

All companies listed above have reported 3 Year CAGR Positive Revenue and all (except Finolex Ind) companies reported 3 Year CAGR Positive Net Profit.

Astral Polytech has the highest Market Capitalization and Supreme Industries has reported highest Sales.

"Any bull market covers a multitude of sins, so there may be all sorts of problems with the current system that we won't see until the bear market comes." – Ron Chernow

Beta of all mentioned companies is less than one indicating less volatility and risk associated in the sector.PE Ratio is mix where few are above and few are below the Sector PE indicating there is good possibility of growth in this sector.

Good returns have been shown by SUPREME and ASTRAL Polytech in past 2 years and 5 years.

Airlines

The civil aviation industry in India has emerged as one of the fastest growing industries in the country during last three years. India has become one of the largest domestic aviation market in the world and is expected to overtake UK to become the third largest air passenger market by 2024.

Listed here are few of the companies of this sector which can be studied and analyzed by the readers for investment and building their portfolio. Some high level detail of the sector and stocks is described below.

S.No.	Company Name	Piotroski Score	Sales (In Cr) Year 2020
1	Interglobe Aviation Ltd (Indigo)	2	35756
2	Spice Jet	1	12374
3	TAAL Enterprises Ltd	6	129
4	Global Vectra Helicorp Ltd.	4	66

"Fundamentalists who say they are not going to pay any attention to the charts are like a doctor who says he's not going to take a patient's temperature." – Bruce Kovner

This sectors has small, mid and large market cap companies.

All companies mentioned above have reported 3 Year CAGR Positive Revenue and TAAL enterprises and Spice jet have reported 3 Year CAGR Positive Net Profit.

INTERGLOBE aviation limited is at the Top on Market Capitalization and Sales.

Good returns have been shown by TAAL INTERPRISES limited in past 1 and 2 years.

Other Airlines have given very average return or negative return to the investors.

Glass and Glass Products

India is the major producer of Glass and Glass Products.

The India container glass market is expected to register a CAGR of 6.78% during the forecast period of 2021-2026. Container glass is a type of glass for the production of glass containers, such as bottles, jars, drinkware, and bowls.

The increased alcohol consumption in India has contributed to the significant increase in the growth rate of the container glass market in India.

Glass industry requires a large number of raw materials. The most important raw material is silica sand which constitutes 75 per cent of the basic materials.

"Discipline has within it the potential for creating future miracles."
– Jim Rohn

Things to Know Before Investing

Listed here are few of the companies of this sector which can be studied and analyzed by the readers for investment and building their portfolio. Some high level detail of the sector and stocks is described below.

S.No.	Company Name	Piotroski Score	Sales (In Cr) Year 2020
1	Asahi India Glass	5	2643
2	Borosil renewables Ltd	5	761
3	Borosil Ltd	8	635
4	La Opala RG	6	270

This sectors has small and mid-market cap companies

All companies listed above have reported 3 Year CAGR Positive Revenue and all (except Asahi India Glass) have reported 3 Year CAGR Positive Net Profit.

ASAHI INDIA GLASS LIMITED holds Top position on Market Capitalization and in Sales.

Beta of all mentioned companies is less than 1 indicating less risk and volatility. PE Ratio is high for most of the companies as compared to Sector PE indicating prices are overrated but investors are ready to pay the CMP.

Outstanding return on investment have been shown by BOROSIL RENEWABLES LIMITED in past 2 years and 5 years.

"It's more important to grow your income than cut your expenses. It's more important to grow your spirit that cut your dreams."
– Robert Kiyosaki

Paint

The domestic paint industry is estimated to be of Rs. 50,000 Crores industry with the decorative paint category constituting almost 75% of this market. The decorative paint market includes multiple categories depending on the nature of the surface like exterior wall paints, interior wall paints, wood finishes, enamels as well as ancillary products like primers, putties, etc.

The industrial paint category constitutes the balance 25% of the paint market and includes a broad array of segments like automotive coatings, marine coatings, packaging coatings, powder coatings, protective coatings, and other general industrial coatings.

Paint Sector is growing at a fast pace and there are many players entering into the market.

Listed here are few of the companies of this sector which can be studied and analyzed by the readers for investment and building their portfolio. Some high level detail of the sector and stocks is described below.

S.No.	Company Name	Piotroski Score	Sales (In Cr) Year 2020
1	Asian Paints	8	20211
2	Berger Paints	6	6365
3	Kansai Nerolac	7	5279
4	Akzo Nobel	8	2661

"There are a million ways to make money in the markets. The irony is that they are all very difficult to find." – Jack D. Schwager

This sectors has mid and large market cap companies

All companies mentioned have 3 Year CAGR Positive Revenue and 3 Year CAGR Positive Net Profit indicating good growth in Revenue and Net Profit for mentioned companies.

ASIAN PAINTS being at the Top on Market Capitalization and in Sales

Beta of all companies is less than 1 indicating less risk and volatility. PE Ratio is mix where some are above and some are below the Sector PE indicating there is good possibility of growth in this sector for many stocks

Good returns have been shown by BERGER and ASIAN PAINTS in past 2 years and 5 years.

Paper

Paper, is considered as a touchstone of socio-economic development. The sector has witnessed a huge change in the structure during the last three decades. Also the low per capita paper consumption in India compared to world's average promises high growth of the sector in future. Moreover, the paper imports have been declining due to tremendous rise in the domestic production, reflecting the self-sufficiency of the sectors over the years. At the same time, the sector also witnessed an upward trend in export growth after liberalization. The rising exports to high, middle, and low-income countries

"Simple can be harder than complex: You have to work hard to get your thinking clean to make it simple. But it's worth it in the end because once you get there, you can move mountains." – Steve Jobs

reflect the sector increasingly becoming self-independent and integrated with the world.

Listed here are few of the companies of this sector which can be studied and analyzed by the readers for investment and building their portfolio. Some high level detail of the sector and stocks is described below.

S.No.	Company Name	Piotroski Score	Sales (In Cr) Year 2020
1	JK Paper	5	3060
2	West Coast Paper	4	2492
3	Emami Paper Mills	5	1515
4	Seshasayee Paper	5	1184

This sectors has small and mid-market cap companies.

All companies mentioned have registered 3 Year CAGR Positive Revenue and all (except Emami Paper Mills) have registered 3 Year CAGR Positive Net Profit.

J K Paper is at the Top on Market Capitalization and Sales.

Beta of most of all high turnover companies is less than 1 indicating less risk and volatility. PE Ratio is high for most of the companies as compared to Sector PE indicating prices are overrated but investors are ready to pay the Current Market Price.

"Graham's wonderful sentence as, an investor needs only two things: cash and courage. Having only one of them is not enough."
– Seth Klarman

Good returns have been shown by JK PAPERS, WESTCOAST PAPERS in past 5 years whereas the return on investment in last 2 years is poor from this sector on most of the stocks.

Textiles

India's textiles sector is one of the oldest industries in the Indian economy, extremely varied, with hand-spun and hand-woven textiles sectors at one end to the sophisticated mills sector on the other end. The power looms/hosiery and knitting sector forms the largest component in the textiles sector. The close linkage of textiles industry to agriculture (for raw materials such as cotton) and the ancient culture and traditions of the country in terms of textiles makes it unique in comparison to other sectors. India's textiles industry produces a wide variety of products suitable for different market segments, both for domestic consumption and for consumption across the world.

The future for the Indian textiles industry looks promising, for the strong domestic consumption as well as export demand. With consumerism and disposable income on the rise, the retail sector has experienced a rapid growth in the past decade. Listed here are few of the companies of this sector which can be studied and analyzed by the readers for investment and building their portfolio. Some high level detail of the sector and stocks is described below.

"Whatever is newly expensive has two attributes: wonderful past returns and, in most cases, lousy future returns." – Robert D. Arnott

S.No.	Company Name	Piotroski Score	Sales (In Cr) Year 2020
1	K P R Mill Ltd	7	3352
2	Page Industries	5	2945
3	Lux Industries	6	1206
4	Rupa & Co	6	974

This sectors has mid and large market cap companies.

All companies, except Rupa and Co have reported 3 Year CAGR Positive Revenue and 3 Year CAGR Positive Net Profit.

PAGE industries limited has the highest Market Capitalization and KPR mills Limited has the highest reported Sales.

Beta of most of all high turnover companies is less than 1 indicating less risk and volatility. PE Ratio is high for most of the companies as compared to Sector PE indicating prices are overrated but investors are ready to pay the CMP.

Good returns have been shown by PAGE industries, KPR Mills limited and Rupa and company in past 2 years and LUX in last 5 years.

Consumer Goods – Electrical

Listed here are few of the companies of this sector which can be studied and analyzed by the readers for investment and building their portfolio. Some high level detail of the sector and stocks is described below.

"Some people get rich studying artificial intelligence. Me, I make money studying natural stupidity." – Carl Icahn

S.No.	Company Name	Piotroski Score	Sales (In Cr) Year 2020
1	Havells India	5	9440
2	Bajaj Electricals	4	4977
3	V-Guard Inds.	5	2516

Havells India and BAJAJ limited have provided good returns in last 2 years and all have provided good returns in last 5 years

Marine Port and Services

This sector has huge growth potential based on the major drivers of growth for this industry like high growth of the marine freight transportation industry and surging demand of containerized and bulk cargo. Increasing global exports, rising customer (Shipping companies) demand, and expansion of new regional trade hubs are the additional factors contributing to accelerated growth.

Emerging trends, which have a direct impact on the dynamics of the marine port and service industry include efficient handling of containers, vessel traffic services (VTS), efficient and up-to-date self-unloading bulk carrier technology, and marine port overall operational efficiency.

Listed here are few of the companies of this sector which can be studied and analyzed by the readers for investment and

"In reality, no one knows what the market will do; trying to predict it is a waste of time, and investing based upon that prediction is a speculative undertaking." – Seth Klarman

building their portfolio. Some high level detail of the sector and stocks is described below.

S.No.	Company Name	Piotroski Score	Sales (In Cr) Year 2020
1	Adani Ports	5	11873
2	Dredging Corp	6	749
3	Gujarat Pipavav	8	735

ADANI PORTS has provided good returns in last 2 years and 5 years.

Refineries & Petro Products/Integrated Oil & Gas/Oil & Gas – Exploration and Production

This sector is the backbone of any economy and is among the eight core industries in India and plays a major role in influencing decision making for all the other important sections of the economy. India's economic growth is closely related to its energy demand, therefore, oil and gas is projected to grow more.

India has always been a major Liquefied Natural Gas (LNG) importer. India's energy demand is expected to increase significantly along with Natural Gas consumption and Diesel.

The growth of this sector is bound to happen as there are other sectors whose growth is depended on Oil and Gas production and consumption.

"Everything I have is for sale, except for my kids and possibly my wife." – Carl Icahn

Listed here are few of the companies of this sector which can be studied and analyzed by the readers for investment and building their portfolio. Some high level detail of the sector and stocks is described below.

S.No.	Company Name	Piotroski Score	Sales (In Cr) Year 2020
1	Reliance Industries	5	596743
2	ONGC	4	396802
3	B P C L	5	284571
4	HPCL	5	269091
5	MRPL	2	50230
6	Oil India Ltd	6	12166

RELIANCE INDUSTRIES has provided good returns in last 2 years and 5 years.

"If you want to know everything about the market, go to the beach. Push and pull your hands with the waves. Some are bigger waves, some are smaller. But if you try to push the wave out when it's coming in, it'll never happen. The market is always right". – Ed Seykota

2.7 Picking the Right Stock in the Stock Market

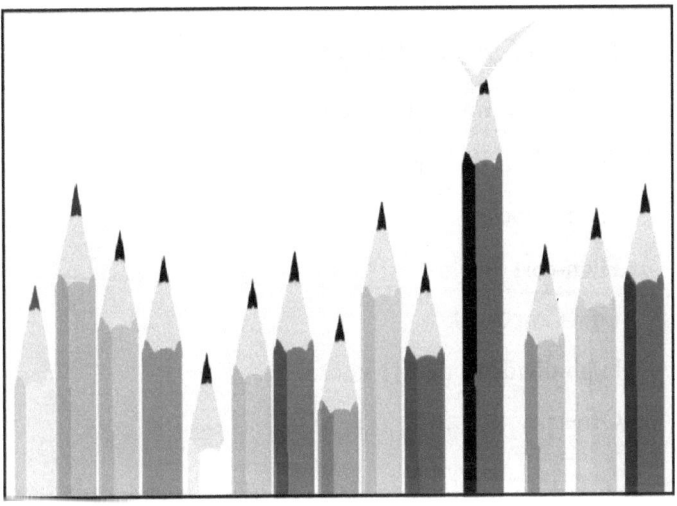

This is the first step when we plan to enter the market. Picking the right stock is a challenging task and it all depends on what we pick and choose from the variety of stocks available in the market. There are 5000 plus stocks available on BSE and 1600 plus stock available on NSE

We have to identify the Equities Stocks into different categories before deciding which one to invest in.

"When purchasing depressed stock in troubled companies, seek out the ones with the superior financial positions and avoid the ones with loads of bank debt." – Peter Lynch

Following categories and a few more can be decided to identify them for investing. Equities Stocks from different categories of Market Cap is to be selected for diversification.

High Growth Stocks

Stable and Value stocks

Low return stocks

Languishing/Loss Making Stocks

Long Term Investment Stock

Short Term Buying Stocks

Penny Stocks

High-cost Stocks

Low-Cost Stocks

High dividend-paying stocks

Others…………..

Now based on the fund available to invest, picking the right stock is the first step that is to be done right.

To remain invested in the market and make a good profit, it is necessary to pick the stocks which are fundamentally strong and will give good returns in the future.

When Investors refer to fundamentally strong Stocks, they are referring to stocks which are good in terms of doing existing business and are established player in their field with good

"I will tell you how to become rich. Close the doors. Be fearful when others are greedy. Be greedy when others are fearful." – Warren Buffett

market share and good financials to support the business.
Fundamentally Strong Player in the Market

Has Good Market Capitalization

Has good volume of Trade

Has Good PE ratio

Has Good Earning Per Share EPS

Making profit consistently since last few years and growing

Consistent Revenue Growth

Has given good dividend in the past

We need to make a list of our stocks which can be chosen for the investment and are fundamentally strong. There are different tools available in the market to pick stocks based on different criterias that we would like to use and filter the stocks. It is recommneded to use the tools to identfy and pick the stocks according to our set criteria.

"Charting is a little like surfing. You don't have to know a lot about the physics of tides, resonance, and fluid dynamics in order to catch a good wave. You just have to be able to sense when its happening and then have the drive to act at the right time." – Ed Seykota

2.8 Technical Analysis of Stock

Checking the fundamentals of the company is paramount and critical to decide on investing. However, the right time to invest is determined by the technical analysis of the Stock.

There is a possibility that the stock may be very good fundamentally nevertheless the trend may be negative for the period. There is a need to refrain from investing in such a

"Thousands of experts study overbought indicators, head-and-shoulder patterns, put-call ratios, the Fed's policy on money supply… and they can't predict markets with any useful consistency, any more than the gizzard squeezers could tell the Roman emperors when the Huns would attack." – Peter Lynch

time period when the time is going to be bad for the script. It is crucial to wait till the stock recovers in an upward trend. Plans for investment can be made once the stock catches on an upward trend.

Similarly, if investment in a fundamentally strong company has already been made and the technical analysis trend says that it will take a deep dive, we can plan to exit from such stocks even at the cost of making some losses. If we are in profit, it is suggested to book profit and exit from such stock for some time. Some will decide to remain invested in such stocks as they invest on long terms basis and would like to continue.

So before buying any stock, it is always preferred to do a technical analysis of the stock.

A candlestick is a way of displaying information about a Stock or an Asset's price movement.

Candlestick charts are one of the most popular components of technical analysis, enabling investors and traders to interpret price information quickly and from just a few price bars.

In Candle Stick, the body, which represents the open-to-close range.

The wick, or shadow, indicates high and low.

The color, which reveals the direction of market movement – a green (or white) body indicates a price increase, while a red (or black) body shows a price decrease

"Technical analysis is a skill that improves with experience and study. Always be a student and keep learning." – John Murphy

Things to Know Before Investing

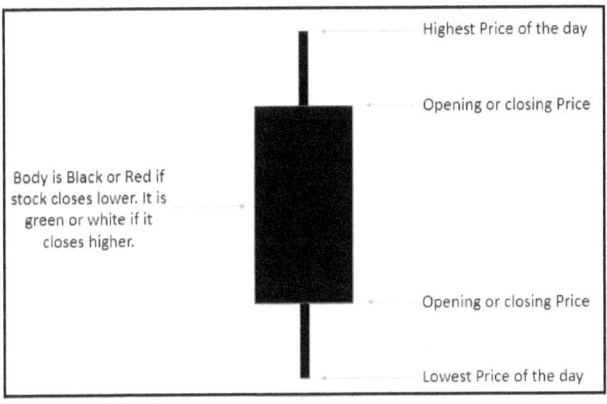

Candlesticks reflect the impact of investor sentiment on security prices. They are frequently used by technical analysts to determine when to enter and exit trades. Candlestick charting is based on a technique developed in Japan in the 1700s. Candlesticks are a suitable technique for trading any liquid financial asset such as stocks, foreign exchange, and futures.

Long white/green candlesticks indicate there is strong buying pressure; this typically indicates that the price is bullish. Long black/red candlesticks indicate there is significant selling pressure. This suggests the price is bearish. A common bullish candlestick reversal pattern referred to as a hammer, forms when the price moves substantially lower after the open, then rallies to close near the high. The equivalent bearish candlestick is known as a hanging man. We will cover some of the candlestick patterns and many others can be explored. There are many websites which the detail of the Technical Analysis and Candle Stick Pattern.

"Charts really are the 'footprint of money." – Fred McAllen

Indecisive Candles

One of the most prominent candlestick signals is called the 'Indecision Candle'.

Indecision candles have a small body (the close price of the candle is near the open price). Also, the body of the candle must be centered within the whole candle range. Finally, the indecision candle must have long wicks protruding from each side of the body, around equal lengths at both ends.

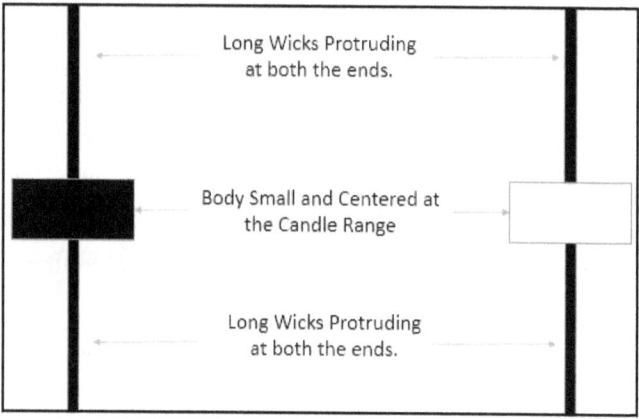

Such Candle Sticks signifies that the price action traders' bulls and the bears were very active to pull it in its own direction. Because there was no winner by the end of the candle's session, the market closes approximately in the same area where it had opened. This type of behavior demonstrates indecisiveness, hence the name indecision candle. An indecision candle indicates a probability of price reversal.

"Every decade or so, dark clouds will fill the economic skies, and they will briefly rain gold." – Warren Buffett

Things to Know Before Investing

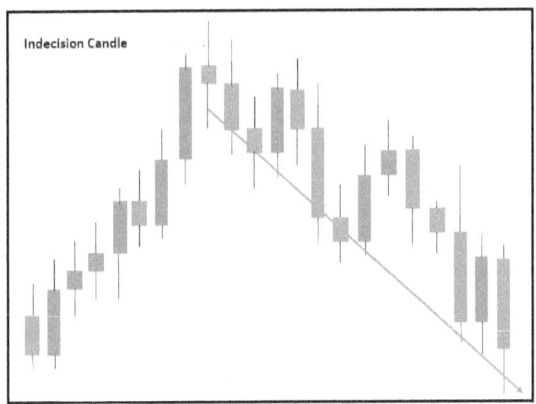

Indecision candles can often be found at the tops and bottoms of trends. They form because the probability of price running into a major reversal area on the chart is expected, like a weekly support or resistance level when the huge orders flood into the market as money exchanges hands.

It can also lead to trend continuance breakout as shown below.

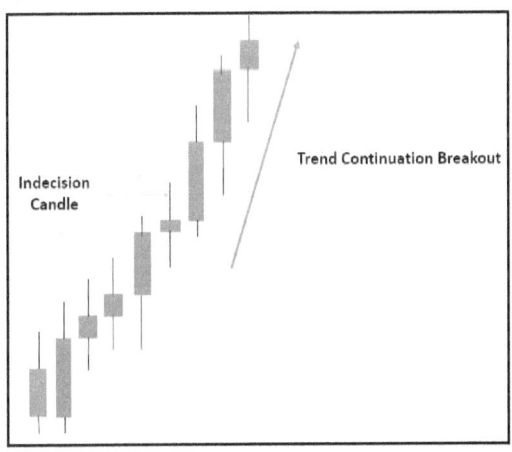

"Keep your eyes on the stars, and your feet on the ground."
– *Theodore Roosevelt*

There are two types of indecision pattern.

The Spinning Top Pattern

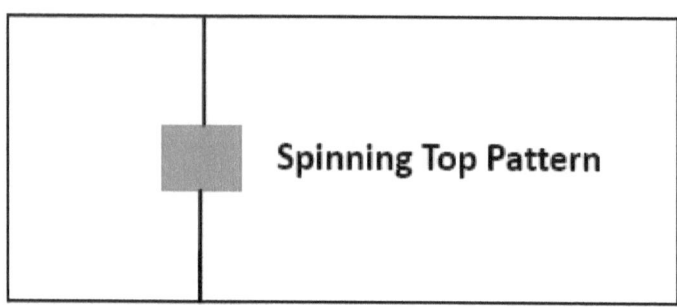

The spinning top pattern is an indecision pattern forming whenever both selling and buying pressure is battling to have control in the market.

There are two ways to recognize a spinning top pattern candlestick.

One, the candle has a long upper and lower shadow and the other is that the candle has a small body.

The spinning top pattern indicates two things.

Firstly, buyers and sellers both are aggressive, trying to take control resulting in upper and lower shadows.

Secondly, looking forward to the end of the session neither of two gains.

The spinning top indicates significant volatility within the market without a clear outcome of the winner any, i.e. buyers or the sellers.

"Remember that the stock market is a manic depressive." – Warren Buffet

The Doji Pattern

Doji pattern, also an indecision pattern that forms whenever both buying and selling pressure is in equilibrium.

Even though Doji is an indecision pattern, there are different importance. There are two types of Doji pattern.

1. Dragonfly Doji

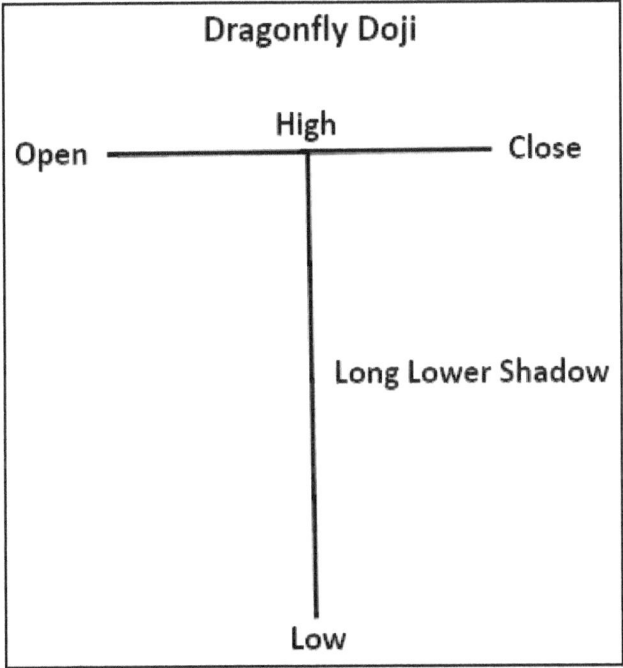

Dragonfly Doji opens and closes close the highs of the range with long lower shadow.

"In the world of business, the people who are most successful are those who are doing what they love." – Warren Buffett

Dragonfly Doji occurs whenever there's a rejection of lower prices while buying pressure steps in to push the market to a higher opening price.

The chart below of the Stock/asset illustrates a Dragonfly Doji occurring at the bottom of a downtrend.

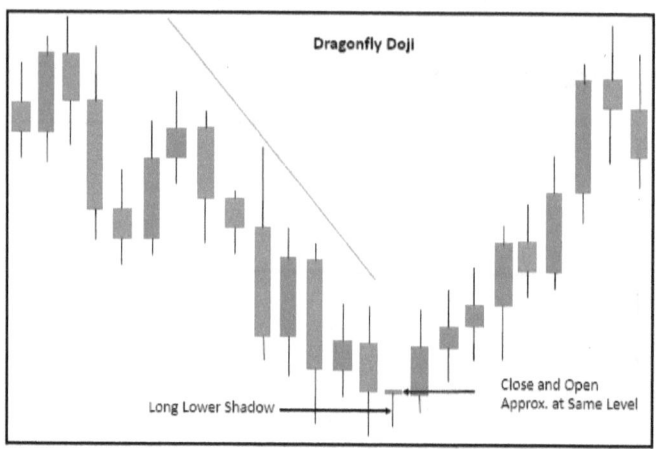

In Chart above, the market began by testing to find where demand would enter the market, found support for the low price, but indicated a possible transition to an uptrend.

2. Gravestone Doji

Gravestone Doji opens and closes, close to the lows of the range having a long upper shadow. Gravestone Doji indicates

> *"You can only become truly accomplished at something you love. Don't make money your goal. Instead, pursue the things you love doing, and then do them so well that people cannot take their eyes off you." – Maya Angelou*

a refusal of higher prices while selling pressure is high pushing the market lower to the opening price.

In the case of this candlestick pattern, the longer the shadow, the more negative is the candle. Thus Doji candle ended the session at the same price at which it had begun.

Looking at the candle, we can interpret the basic underlying psychology of the candle is to reflect a session that ends in indecision.

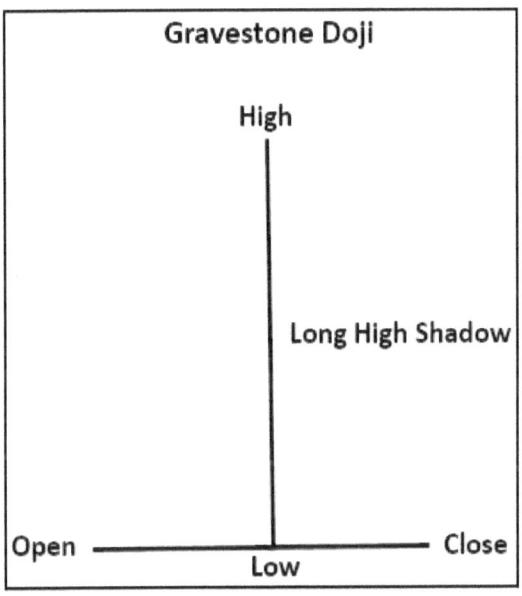

The Japanese candlestick states that a gravestone doji represents the gravestones of the bulls. Gravestone Doji is a candlestick where the open, low, and close are at the low of the day. The

"The true investor… will do better if he forgets about the stock market and pays attention to his dividend returns and to the operating results of his companies." – Jack Bogle

Gravestone Doji is a bearish formation. The psychology behind this candle is that the bulls pushed the security up to an unsustainable level and then the bears pulled it back down to its low by the end of the session.

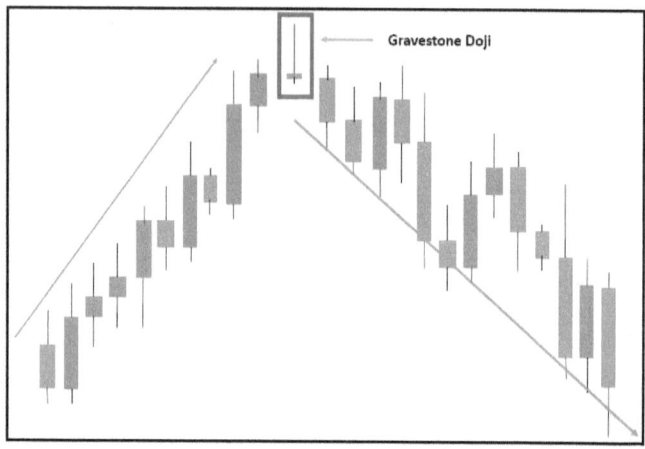

Bullish Harami

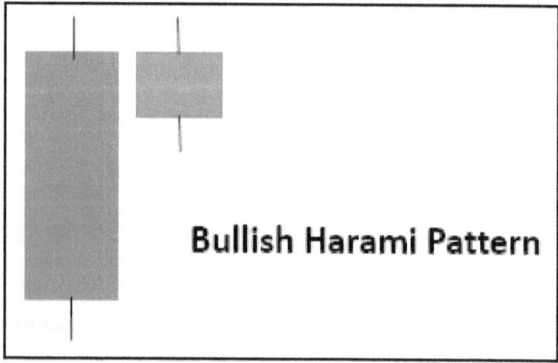

"Don't think that you know more than the market; no one does. And don't act on insights that you think are your own but are usually shared by millions of others." – Jack Bogle

A Bullish harami pattern indicates two things. Firstly, the first candle showing the buying pressure while the candle closes bullishly. Secondly, the second next candle indicates indecision while both buying and selling pressure looks like.

The bullish harami works well as a continuation pattern within the uptrend.

Bullish Engulfing

The Bullish Engulfing Candlestick Pattern is a bullish reversal pattern, usually occurring at the bottom of a downtrend. The pattern consists of two Candlesticks as shown.

The image below depicts the bullish engulfing pattern appearing at the bottom of a downtrend

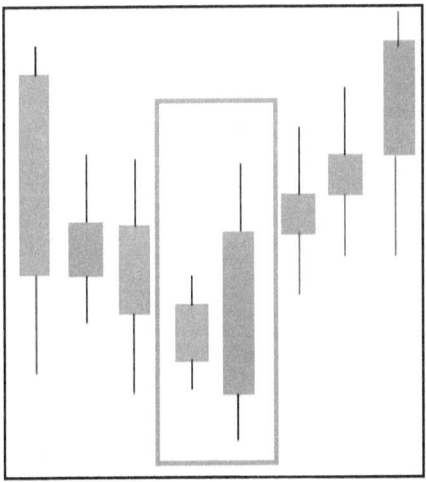

"Rely on the ordinary virtues that intelligent, balanced human beings have relied on for centuries: common sense, thrift, realistic expectations, patience, and perseverance." – Jack Bogle

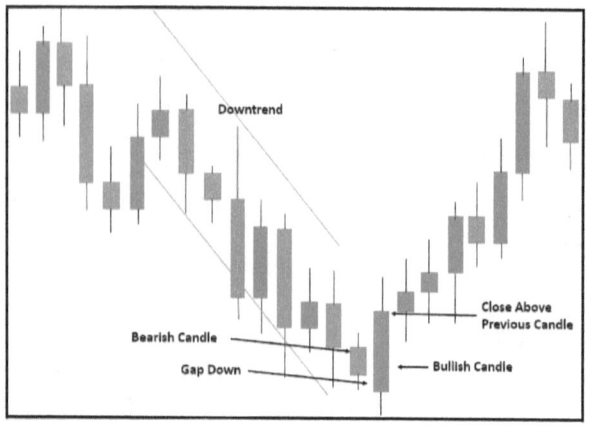

The pattern involves two candles with the second candle completely engulfing the body of the previous red candle.

The bullish engulfing candle appears at the bottom of a downtrend and indicates a surge in buying pressure. The bullish engulfing pattern generally triggers a reversal in trend.

The Morning Star

Three, candlesticks sequenced in a particular order makes the morning star pattern. The pattern is encircled in the chart below.

The morning star is a bullish candlestick pattern and also a downtrend reversal pattern. The pattern is formed by combining 3 candlesticks. The morning star appears at the bottom end of a downward trend. In the chart below the morning, star is encircled.

"If you can dream it, you can do it." – Walt Disney

Things to Know Before Investing

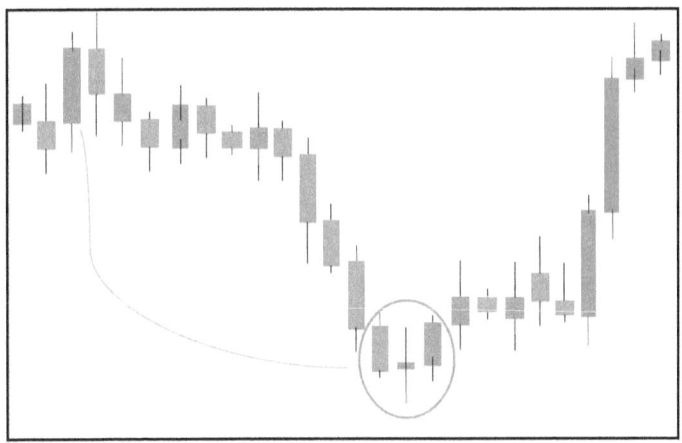

The Bearish Harami

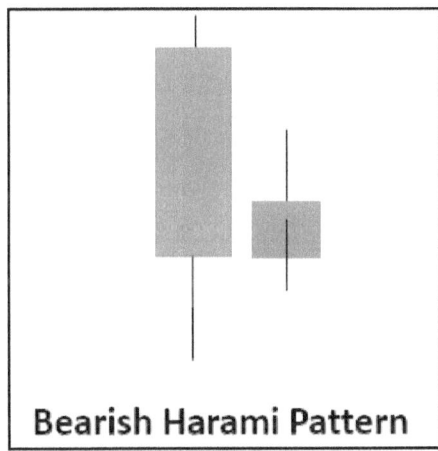

Bearish Harami indicates strong selling pressure and indecision from both (buying and selling) pressure is alike.

"Do not wait; the time will never be just right. Start where you stand, and work with whatever tools you may have at your command, and better tools will be found as you go along." – George Herbert

Bearish harami works as a continuing pattern. There are two ways to indicate a bearish harami. One, the first candle is larger and bearish compare with the second one, and the second the following candle shas a small range and body.

The Evening Star

The evening star is a bearish equivalent of the morning star. The evening star appears at the top end of an uptrend. Like the morning star, the evening star is a three candle formation and evolves over three trading sessions.

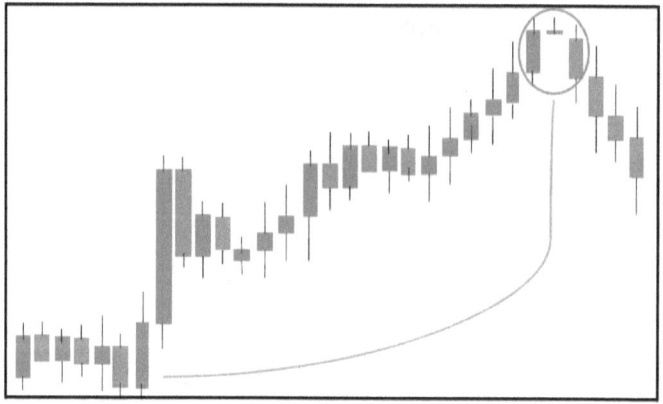

The Gaps

A gap up opening indicates the buyer's excitement.

Buyers are willing to buy stocks at a price higher than the previous day's close. Hence, the stocks open way beyond the

"You can have it all. You just can't have it all at one time."
– Oprah Winfrey

Things to Know Before Investing

previous day's close. For example, consider the closing price of a stock at Rs. 400. In the evening, the company announces a bonus or new big contract deal sign up. The next day morning the buyers are willing to buy the stock at a higher price. This leads to stock price jumping to Rs. 440 directly. This means though there was no trading activity between Rs. 400 and Rs. 440, the stock jumped to Rs. 440. This is called a gap up opening. Gap up opening refers to bullish sentiment.

In the following image, the green arrows point to gap up openings.

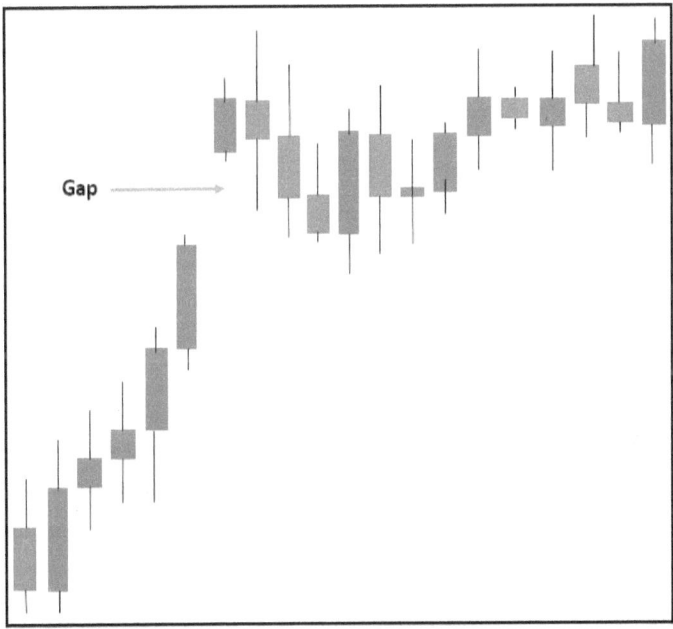

"It's not whether you're right or wrong that's important, but how much money you make when you're right and how much you lose when you're wrong." – George Soros

Gap down opening

Similar to gap up opening, a gap down opening shows the excitement and enthusiasm of the bears. The bears are so willing to sell, that they are ready to sell at a price lower than the previous day's close.

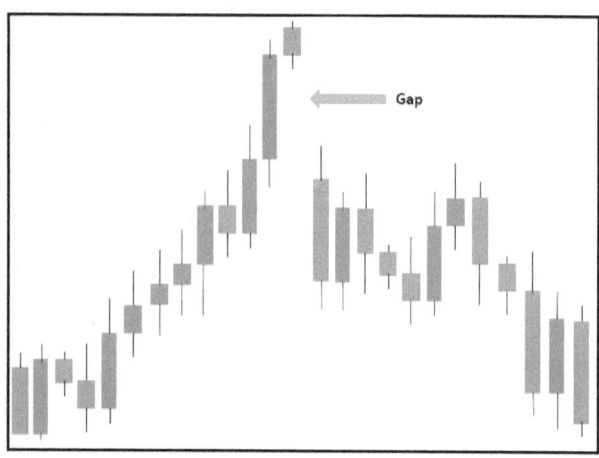

Trend Reversal

Double Top

A double top is a highly bearish technical reversal pattern that forms after an asset reaches a high price consecutive times with a moderate decline between the two highs. A double top signals a trend change in an asset class.

As its name implies, the pattern is made up of two consecutive peaks that are roughly equal, with a moderate low in-between.

"Returns matter a lot. It's our capital." – Abigail Johnson

Things to Know Before Investing

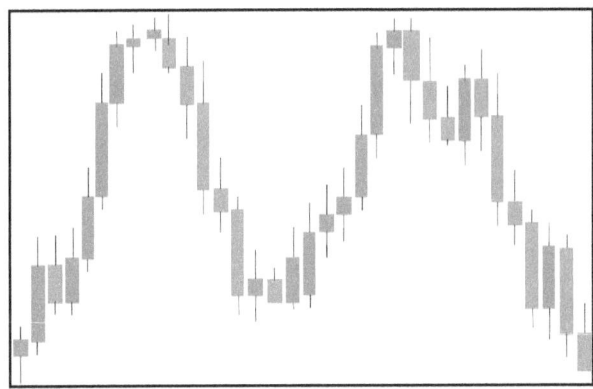

Double Bottom

A double bottom is a highly bullish technical reversal pattern that forms after an asset reaches to a low price consecutive times with a moderate-high between the two highs. A double bottom signals a trend change in an asset class.

As its name implies, the pattern is made up of two consecutive lows that are roughly equal, with a moderate-high in-between.

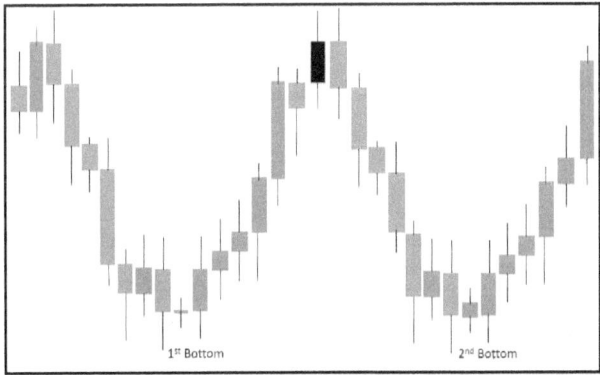

"It's not how much money you make, but how much money you keep, how hard it works for you, and how many generations you keep it for."
– Robert Kiyosaki

Head and Shoulder

The head and shoulders chart pattern is primarily a price reversal pattern. It helps to identify an upcoming trend reversal after a trend has seemingly exhausted itself. It indicates that an uptrend has ended. The pattern appears as a baseline, consisting of three peaks in which the two peaks outside are close in height whereas the one on the middle is the highest. It resembles a distinct, 'left shoulder', a 'head' and a 'right shoulder'.

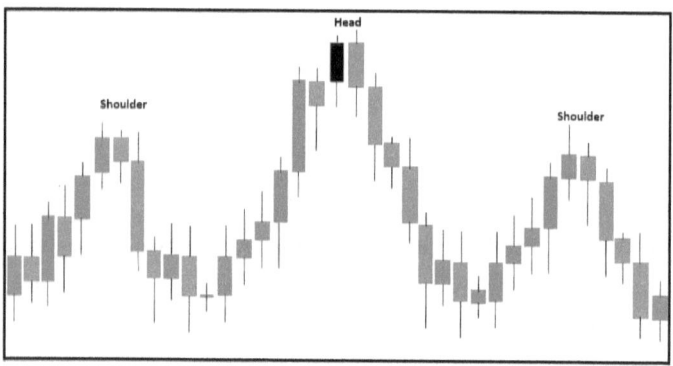

Inverted Head and Shoulder Pattern

The inverse or inverted head and shoulders pattern is the opposite of the regular head and shoulders pattern. The inverted pattern appears when the price of a stock falls to a trough before it rises again. The pattern reappears when the stock price falls below the prior trough and rises again before a final drop. But the rise is not as far or as much as the second trough. After making the final trough, the stock price again

"Know what you own, and know why you own it." – Peter Lynch

begins heading upwards, which is close to the top of the previous troughs.

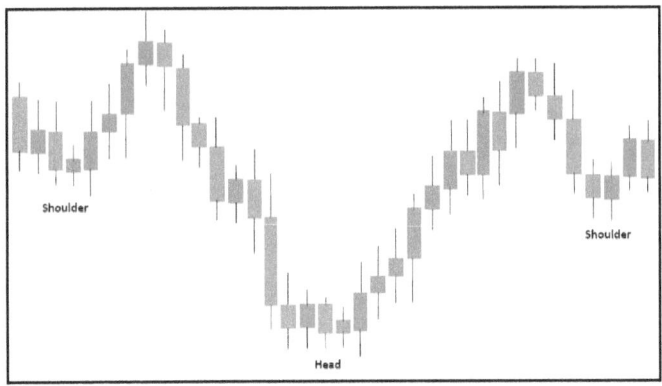

Accumulation/Distribution Indicator (A/D)

Accumulation/distribution is a cumulative indicator that uses volume and price to assess whether a stock is being accumulated or distributed. The accumulation/distribution measure tries to find and identify divergences between the stock price and volume flow. This provides an insight into how strong a trend is going to be. If the price is rising but the indicator is falling this indicates that buying or accumulation volume may not be able to support the price rise and a price decline could be forthcoming.

Accumulation Distribution looks into the proximity of closing prices to their highs or lows to determine if accumulation or distribution is occurring in the market. The proximity value

The four most dangerous words in investing are, it's different this time." – Sir John Templeton

is multiplied by volume to give more weight to moves with higher volume.

The accumulation/distribution line gauges supply and demand by looking at the price closure within the period's range and then multiplying that by volume.

The **A/D indicator** is cumulative, meaning one period's value is added or subtracted from the last.

A rising A/D line helps confirm a rising price trend.

A falling A/D line helps confirm a price downtrend.

If the price is rising but A/D is falling, it signals underlying weakness and a potential decline in price.

If the price of an asset is falling but A/D is rising, it signals underlying strength and the price may start to rise.

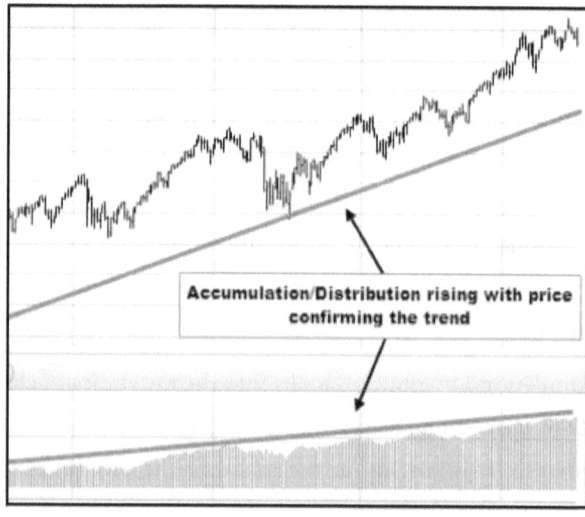

"Trade What's Happening… Not What You Think Is Gonna Happen."
– Doug Gregory

How this indicator works

The actual value of the Accumulation Distribution is inconsequential. Concentrate on its direction.

When both price and Accumulation Distribution are making higher peaks and higher troughs, then up trend is likely to continue.

When both price and Accumulation Distribution are making lower peaks and lower troughs, the downtrend is likely to continue.

If during a trading range, the Accumulation Distribution is rising, then accumulation may be taking place and is a warning of an upward break out.

If during a trading range, the Accumulation Distribution is falling, then the distribution may be taking place and is a warning of a downward breakout.

The Accumulation Distribution Line only looks at the level of the close relative to the high-low range for a given period (day, week, and month). The AD line ignores the change from one period to the next. With this formula, a security could gap down and close significantly lower, but the Accumulation Distribution Line would rise if the close were above the midpoint of the high-low range.

When price continues to make higher peaks and Accumulation Distribution fails to make a higher peak, then up trend is likely to stall or fail. This is known as a negative divergence.

"Buy a stock the way you would buy a house. Understand and like it such that you'd be content to own it in the absence of any market."
– Warren Buffett

When price continues to make lower troughs and Accumulation Distribution fails to make lower troughs, the downtrend is likely to stall or fail. This is known as a positive divergence.

Support Level and Resistance Level

The concepts of level support and resistance are two of the most highly discussed attributes of technical analysis. A the process of analyzing the chart patterns, these terms are used by investors and traders to refer to price levels on charts that tend to act as barriers, preventing the price of an asset from getting pushed in a particular direction.

Technical analysts use support and resistance levels to identify price points on a chart where the probabilities favor a pause or reversal of a prevailing trend.

Support occurs where a downtrend is expected to pause due to a concentration of demand whereas Resistance occurs where an uptrend is expected to pause, due to a concentration of supply.

Support and Resistance are the most commonly used terms in the Stock market as this indicates entry and exit on the stock. If we are holding stock and if it is in an upward trend and its resistance level is higher, we will plan to hold the stock till it reaches around the resistance level. If we do not hold this stock, we may plan to buy it and make a profit.

"You can't produce a baby in one month by getting nine women pregnant." – Warren Buffett

Things to Know Before Investing

Support and Resistance level is decided on the past data and has been it is found that it gives the correct indication most of the time and hence it is referred to most before taking any decision about entry and exit of stock.

In short, Support is a price level where a downtrend can be expected to pause due to a concentration of high demand or buying interest. As the price of assets or securities drops, demand for the shares increases, thus forming the support line. Meanwhile, resistance zones arise due to selling interest when prices have increased to a certain level.

Once an area or zone of support or resistance is reached, the price levels can serve as entry or exit points. Once price reaches a point of support or resistance, the two possibility arises, either it will bounce back away from the support or resistance level, or it will violate the price level and continue in its direction, till it reaches the next support or resistance level.

"When we own portions of outstanding businesses with outstanding managements, our favorite holding period is forever." – Warren Buffett

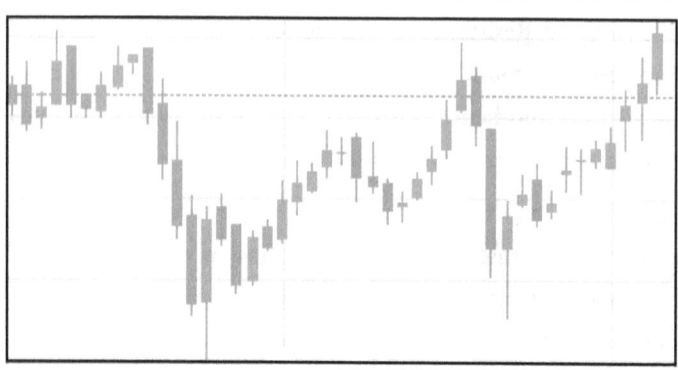

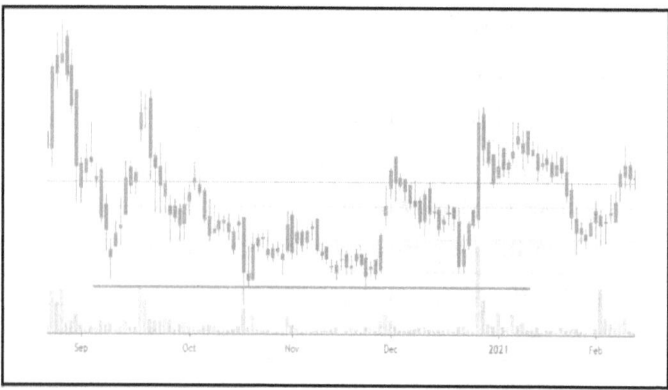

Pivot Points

A pivot point is a technical analysis indicator used to determine support and resistance levels. A pivot point is calculated based on Open, High, Low, and Close Data.

Generally, Pivot Levels are calculated based on Classic, Camarilla, or Fibonacci formulae.

"Do not take yearly results too seriously. Instead, focus on four or five-year averages." – Warren Buffett

If the market trades above the pivot point in the following period, it is usually evaluated as a bullish sentiment, whereas trading below the pivot point is seen as bearish.

Pivot points are mostly used in intra-day indicators for stocks, trading futures, and commodities.

These Pivot Points are theoretical support and resistance levels based on the previous day's open, high, low, and close values: PP, R1, R2, R3, S1, S2, and S3.

PP is the Pivot Point, R1, R2, and R3 are resistance levels, and S1, S2, and S3 are support levels.

Classic Pivot Points

This is a simple average of the high, low, and close. The first and most significant level of support (S1) and resistance (R1) is obtained by recognition of the upper and the lower halves of the prior trading range, defined by the trading above the pivot point (HP), and below it (P − L).

Camarilla Pivot Points

Camarilla pivot point formula is the improved form of the classic pivot point formula. This formula uses the range of the given time frame, daily, weekly, monthly, etc. Camarilla equations take the previous day's high, low and close as input

"The business schools reward difficult complex behavior more than simple behavior, but simple behavior is more effective."
— Warren Buffett

and generate levels of intraday support and resistance based on pivot points.

Fibonacci Pivot Points

Fibonacci Pivot Points start just the same as Standard Pivot Points. From the base Pivot Point, Fibonacci multiples of the high-low differential are added to form resistance levels and subtracted to form support levels.

"Opportunities come infrequently. When it rains gold, put out the bucket, not the thimble." – Warren Buffett

2.9 The Power of Compounding

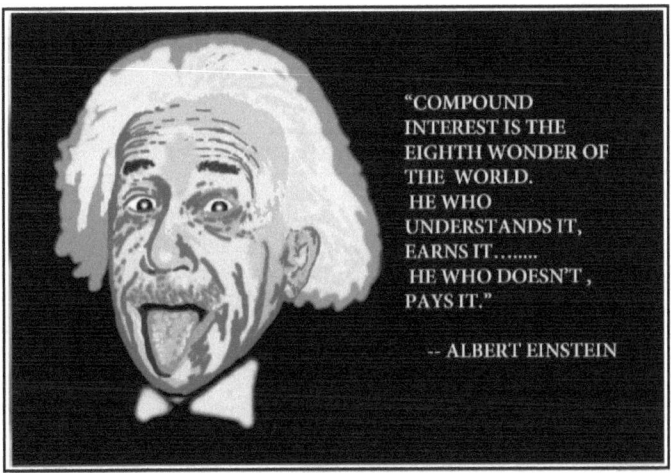

"COMPOUND INTEREST IS THE EIGHTH WONDER OF THE WORLD. HE WHO UNDERSTANDS IT, EARNS IT........ HE WHO DOESN'T, PAYS IT."

-- ALBERT EINSTEIN

Mathematically speaking, compounding is defined as, 'the increase in the value of an investment, due to the interest earned on the principal, as well as the accumulated interest.'

Simply put, it is a strategy that makes our money work for us. It could be regarded as a powerful tool to grow our wealth. We can use the power of compounding to plan our future goals, such as retirement.

"It is incredible how rich you can get by not being perfect."
– Larry Hite

Simple interest means we earn interest on our principal. But with compound interest, we earn interest on the principal amount as well as the accumulated interest amount over successive periods. Over time, this interest snowballs into a substantial amount.

If Amount of Rs. 5000 is invested per month for 30 years and Rate of Interest is 10% PA. Following will the return based on compounding.

Years	5	10	15	20	25	30
Expected amount Rs. (in lakhs)	3.9	10.3	20.9	38.3	66.9	114
Amount invested Rs. (in lakhs)	3	6	9	12	15	18
Wealth Gain Rs. (in lakhs)	0.9	4.3	11.9	26.3	51.9	96

Here are the 3 key rules of investment that helps us to get the true benefit of compounding

Starting Early

There is nothing like starting early to make the most of compounding.

If we start investing from the time we start earning, it will make a solid base for us that will enable our wealth to grow exponentially over time period.

"Trend following is an exercise in observing and responding to the ever-present moment of now." – Ed Seykota

Discipline

If we wish to create a healthy portfolio, we must define our financial goals and be regular in our investments. Knowing our priority and understanding the importance of being disciplined, would pay off later. Being disciplined and developing the habit of investing regularly will help us to create wealth.

Be patient

The patience required for investing is a vital part of financial discipline and shows how well we can check and control our emotional state, fear, and greed, and manage money to achieve the goal.

Being patient with our investment means that we have selected the asset to invest in and we need not bother with the short-term volatility of the market and stock and remain invested for the long-term.

Patience in Stock Market pays off. A lot of us wish for quick returns and do not realize that it is the long-term investments that powerfully reap from the concept of compounding. We have to allow our Investment to grow at its own pace without meddling with it from time to time.

Years of dedicated investment on our part will render a strong and healthy lump sum capital at the end.

"Longevity is the key to success." – Ed Seykota

2.10 Attitude for Success

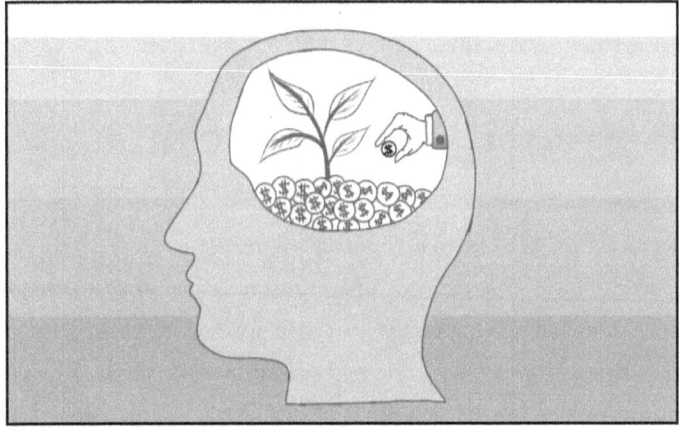

Stock Market provides an opportunity to everyone but it is only encashed by people with positive attitude.

It takes several tests over a significantly large time duration to shape one into a successful investor.

Those who cannot bear the losses and get negative about the stock market very soon, tend to abandon after losing their hard-earned money.

To remain invested and make a profit in the Stock Market, one needs:

"Aim for the moon. If you miss, you may hit a star." – W. Clement Stone

Positive Attitude and Optimistic View

Positive Thinking and a Positive Attitude are prerequisites when it comes to investment in the stock market, especially since there is a high chance of losing on some of the Equities we may buy and the possibility of this happening is also high when we are in the initial phase of learning the nuances of investment and trading.

Perseverance

Perseverance can be summed up to mean how much we are committed to our goal. Success is the fruit of the tree of perseverance. There is not one example in the entire human race that is an exception. Perseverance involves moving on from a failure without losing the enthusiasm to face more failures. Additionally, it enhances the goal's value for us and intensifies our motivation level. It leads us to wonderful findings and broadens our knowledge about ourself and our goals.

It is a well-established fact that success is not achieved overnight. There is no such thing in the world as getting rich and becoming accomplished fast. The journey towards success is slow and precarious at times. It takes hard work and time to build up and makes us solely responsible for our progress. **The stock market is no different.**

"You just can't beat the person who never gives up." – Babe Ruth

Patience

Although the best investors and traders understand the importance of patience, it is one of the most difficult skills to master as an investor and trader. The patience required for investing is a vital part of financial discipline and shows how well we can check emotional state, greed, and manage money to achieve the goal. Being patient with our investment means that once we have selected the asset to invest in, we should not be bothered by short-term volatility in the value of the investment and stay invested for the long-term. The idea here is to select worthy assets at a reasonably good price. Patience is required both at the entry point and also at the exit.

Buying anything in hurry may lead to buying at a higher cost and in the same way selling in hurry will lead to missing the high profit.

It is of utmost importance for any investor to lay the groundwork of the stock before investing, in addition to studying the technicalities of the stock before making an exit.

Patient investing is very similar to fishing. We need to wait to get the result.

Craving to Learn

Investing in the stock market involves study, analysis, research and interpretation of the market trends, conditions, and

"I don't believe in failure. It's not failure if you enjoyed the process."
– Oprah Winfrey

dynamics. There are many factors that affect the stock market and prices of the script like monetary policies, economic growth, etc. It means that if we do not analyze market facts, we cannot make a sound investment decision to purchase stocks in the industries that are performing well or avoid stocks from an industry facing tough economic times.

Stock Market gives opportunity to those who keep learning and increasing their awareness about the market. This is a great place to learn about companies, Stock Market and their Products, how to invest, and many more. As a common adage goes, **Learning never stops**, and it is true for the stock market as well.

Keep learning and investing.

"Michael Marcus taught me one other thing that is absolutely critical: You have to be willing to make mistakes regularly; there is nothing wrong with it. Michael taught me about making your best judgment, being wrong, making your next best judgment, being wrong, making your third best judgment, and then doubling your money." – Bruce Kovner

Chapter 3: Planning and Execution for Investment

3.1 Goal Setting

Our acquaintance with money starts at a very early age when we observe our parents buying chocolates and other stuff in exchange for money. Then, when we start going to school, we start observing the payment of school fees and that of transportation fees for the school van.

Around the same time, we get a piggy bank to start collecting money to meet petty expenses like buying sports item or similar things. Piggybank sets the tone for investment and makes us

"Tell me who your heroes are and I'll tell you who you'll turn out to be." – Warren Buffett

realize the importance of investment and money. Most of the times, the amount collected in a piggy bank is not sufficient to meet the required expenses and we need to add extra money to it to buy something that we desire.

Then we start getting pocket money for some time. Later, we come on to a stage where we have to start thinking about education loans or bike loans. The challenges start multiplying when we start earning, as our commitments and obligations start increasing.

This is also the time when every working professional begins to understand the importance of investments to meet the major expenses which are bound to come.

Our investment planning and its execution at the early age of employment sets the tone for the future and retirement when we would not in a position to earn.

The decisions made during the professional, working phase of life culminate in either a comfortable post-retirement life or a constant struggle to make the ends meet.

Investment goals generally depend on Income, Age, and the Outlook as planned and foreseen.

Depending on the income, age, and outlook we have, investment planning and goal setting is done.

Income provides the option to start investing and hence investment goals become important as we plan for it. The first employment forces us to start investing, for saving tax under

"If you set your goals ridiculously high and it's a failure, you will fail above everyone else's success." – James Cameron

different sections. It is this period of life when our goal-setting should also be done so that there is balance in our day-to-day and major expenses and the regular investments that have to be done for the future.

Age is another factor that decides and dictates our tendencies in investment. There can be three categories of people as per their age, with slightly different goals, and priorities in life.

Young folks are not much bothered about investment as they are focused on career building, whereas the middle-aged are focused on family building. Old people mostly tend to look for peace and continuance of status quo if everything is in control and as per plan, else they are struggling to make the ends meet if proper investment planning was not done during early or middle age.

Our outlook dictates the priorities we have, and the choices we make to lead our life, which in turn, governs the way we live, our lifestyle, and the wealth we would create. Our career planning and expectations decide most of these and people who are serious about bettering their career for a better lifestyle and high earning do well at all the fronts, whereas others struggle to cover the day-to-day expenses and to make out a living.

Investment goals become moving targets for many of us due to various unexpected challenges we may come across in our life,

"The greatest glory in living lies not in never falling, but in rising every time we fall." – Nelson Mandela

like loss of a job, no salary increments to cover the inflation, health issues, and expenses of elderly parents and others.

Fortunately, it's never too late to become an investor. We may be in our late 30s or 40s but we can always plan for the investment for our old age and retirement.

That said, it is still obvious that those who start investing early hold a major advantage, as their investment starts giving results early and make them financially free at an early stage of life and career.

So, goal setting becomes important and imperative for everyone and especially for working-class people. Investment goal engages our thought processes in the right and positive direction, generates accountability and invokes discipline to remain on track. It motivates us on non-financial goals too in a positive way, which can improve health and mental outlook.

It also gives us an incentive for the sacrifices that are to be made and a drive to stick to the regulated budgets. It also makes us understand that any delay or failure will have a direct and immediate impact on our future planning, aspirations, wealth creation, and lifestyle.

Goal Setting has been majorly divided into two types when it comes to investment.

1. Financial Goal Setting
2. Process Goal Setting for Investment

"Someone's sitting in the shade today because someone planted a tree a long time ago." – Warren Buffett

Financial Goal Setting

Following can be part of our financial goal setiing.

Building a corpus for the higher education of children

Meeting unforeseen, emergency expenses

Accumulating for Short Team Goals

Buying a car, luxury car, house, etc.

Planning for accumulating retirement fund

Stock Market Process Goal

Process goal for Stock Market can be set as some of the following points:

I will invest certain fixed amount every month.

I will only withdraw the profit.

I will remain invested and will not sell my Equities unless it is required.

I will sell my Stock when I get a profit of XYZ percent.

I will reinvest my profit in the market for exponential growth.

I will invest only once/twice a month.

I will not look at my Stock investment every day.

I will make plan on my investment as below

The question should not be how much I will profit on this trade! The true question is; will I be fine if I don't profit from this trade."
– Yvan Byeajee

Large Cap   – X percent

Mid Cap   – Y percent

Small-Cap   – Z Percent

No Investment in Penny Stock

If there is any withdrawal from Stock Market for an urgent reason, the same will be reinvested in the market.

Certain percentage of salary will be for investment and no sale of stock will be done in upcoming 10 (XYZ) years.

Review of investment will be done monthly. Stock Market Process Goal is very important which needs to be prepared at individual level based on priorities and purpose of investment.

> *"It's very difficult for any particular segment of the stock market to sustain superior performance. The watch word for our financial markets is, "reversion to the mean" i.e. what goes up must come down, and it's true more often than you can imagine." – John C. Bogle*

3.2 Plan and Prepare to Invest in the Stock Market

Once our goal is set and we are ready to invest, we need to make a plan on how, what, when, how much to invest. This will set the foundation for our next action.

Planning is the key to successful investing. Investing in stocks without any knowledge or preparation is a sure way to lose our capital. If we invest our money on impulse, we are bound to cut a sorry figure. But if we plan and prepare to invest with the right strategy our investment and portfolio will grow exponentially. Proper planning will help us to make the right

"It is better to fail in originality than to succeed in imitation."
– *Herman Melville*

kind of portfolio and will help us make the right decision to buy or sell the stocks. It will also help us in making our long term and short term goals. Regular monitoring of the plan will also give us opportunity to make course corrections based on changing market scenarios. There are simple and some straightforward ways of preparing for investment which gives a good opportunity and a chance to come out like a winner.

Planning and preparing the investment approach will make the things fall in right place from the initial phase itself.

Fundamental Analysis and Technical Analysis is a must for any investment to be done. Below is the detail on both topics.

Fundamental Analysis

Fundamental analysis has been one of the most rewarding analyses in the stock market. In fundamental analysis, we evaluate security by using economic, financial, qualitative, and quantitative factors to determine its intrinsic value. It is believed that macroeconomic and microeconomic factors can affect a security's value. These factors can be economic conditions, industry conditions, financial conditions, and management's proficiency. The main motive while doing a fundamental analysis should be to evaluate a security's intrinsic value and compare it with the current stock price of the security, thus determining if the security is undervalued or overvalued.

"If you genuinely want something, don't wait for it -- teach yourself to be impatient." – Gurbaksh Chahal

Understand the Company

It is crucial to understand the company in which we intend to invest. It will give us insight as to how the company is performing. Understanding whether the company is making the right decisions towards its future goal or not, helps in deciding if we should hold or sell the stock. Visiting its website and learning about the company, its management, its promoters, its products and financials is a good way to get the basic information about the company.

Market Capitalization

Market cap is a shorter and commonly used version of the term' Market Capitalization'. It means the total value of all the shares of a company combined.

Market Cap = Price of one share x Total number of shares issued by the company.

Market cap is a way of calculating the worth of a company. A higher market cap generally means bigger worth of the company, while a lower market cap indicates that the company is of lower worth and has to grow.

Study the Financial Reports of the Company

Once we have a high-level idea of the company, we can start analyzing its financials such as balance sheet, profit-loss

---

"I didn't fail the test. I just found 100 ways to do it wrong."
– Benjamin Franklin

statements, cash flow statements, operating cost, revenue, expenses, etc. We can evaluate its compounded annual growth rate (CAGR), sales and if the net profit has been increasing for the last few years, it can be considered a healthy sign for the company and such companies can be marked for investment.

Balance Sheet

It offers a snapshot of a company's health. It tells how much a company owns (assets) and how much it owes (liabilities). Assets comprise current assets (i.e. cash, inventories, and account receivables) and fixed assets (i.e., plant & equipment, property). Liabilities too have got two kinds which include current liabilities (i.e. obligations to be paid within a year time) and long-term liabilities (i.e., obligations such as debt to be paid in more than a year time).

Cash Flow Statements

It shows how much cash flows into and out of a company over the quarter or year period.

Ratios

The most frequently used ratios which provide insight into a company are:

Liquidity Analysis

"If you are bearish or bullish long enough, you will eventually be right" – *Unknown*

Current Ratio = Current assets/Current liabilities

Quick Ratio = Current assets - Inventories/Current liabilities

Value Ratios

1. **Earnings Per Share (EPS):** It denotes the amount of earnings for each outstanding share. It is calculated as net earnings divided by total outstanding shares.

2. **Price-to-Earnings Ratio (P/E Ratio):** It indicates whether a stock is priced relatively high/low to its earning and a company with a high P/E ratio is believed to be expensive and vice-versa. It is calculated as the market price of a share divided by earning per share. However, the P/E ratio does not tell the full story. Normally, companies with high earning growth are traded at higher P/E values than companies with a moderate growth rate. Accordingly, if the company is growing or expected to grow rapidly, the current market price might not seem so expensive.

3. **Price-to-Book Ratio (P/B Ratio):** A price to book ratio is used to compare a stock's market value to its book value. It is calculated as the current share price of a share divided by the book value per share. It can also be calculated as the total market capitalization of the company divided by all the shareholders' Stock.

"Opportunities always look bigger after they have passed." – Unknown

4. **Net Profit Margin:** It measures how much the company keeps in earnings out of every rupee for their earnings. It is calculated as net profit after tax divided by net sales in the given year.

5. **Return on Stock (RoE):** It is a measure of how well a company uses reinvested earnings to generate additional money. It is calculated as net income divided by Stock capital.

6. **Return on Capital Employed (RoCE):** It is a measure of the returns that a company is realizing from its capital. It is calculated as net profit divided by capital employed.

7. **Debt to Asset Ratio:** This tells how much a company relies on debt to finance assets.

8. **Debt to Stock Ratio:** It measures a company's financial leverage.

9. **Operating Cash Flow Margin:** This is a measure to know whether current cash flow can support the expenses.

10. **Sales to Cash Flow Ratio:** An indicator of the financial strength of the company. The ratio looks at sales concerning cash flow, the higher the value of this ratio, the stronger the company.

11. **Profit After Tax (PAT):** It arrived at by deducting expenditures (cost of materials, manufacturing

"There comes a point when you stand in the rain and you get so wet, you can't get any wetter." – Unknown

expenses, overheads, interest, and depreciation) from income (net sales plus other income) and providing for taxation and investment allowances reserve on the amount.

12. **Earnings before Interest, Tax, Depreciation, and Amortization (EBITDA):** It is found out by deducting operational expenditures from sales.
13. **Dividend Yield** = Annual dividends per share/ Market price per share

Find the Peer Group Companies

The Company we want to invest in must be one of the best among its peers. Try to find a company which is performing better than the other companies. It should have better prospects, upcoming projects, new plants, etc.

Analyze the Prospects

Fundamental analysis is most effective when we want to stay invested long term. Invest in those companies whose products will still be useful after 15–25 years down the line.

Review all the Aspects from Time to Time

Do not invest in a company and forget about it. Stay updated about the company you have invested in. We should be

"Rich people makes money when the stock market goes up, rich people makes even more money when the stock market goes down." – Unknown

updated about all its news and financial performance. Sell the security if there is a problem in the company.

Technical Analysis of Stocks

Mathematics, data, and statistical techniques are fast taking over and changing the world and decisions. Technical analysis is used by most investors and traders. The fundamentals of technical analysis are fairly easy to understand. Once we know it, we can easily understand how to do technical analysis of stocks.

In technical analysis, we study chart patterns and statistical figures to understand market trends and pick stocks accordingly.

If we analyze the stock price movement, we will see fluctuations in the price every day but if we see it over a period of time, we will see trends and patterns emerging. The study of these chart patterns and trends in stock prices is called technical analysis of stocks. When we learn technical analysis of stocks, we shall be able to forecast the movement of stock price to a great extent.

Technical analysts believe that historical price trends tend to repeat over time. So, based on the historical stock charts, we look at price and volume information, and then using trends, we try to figure out how the stock's price may move in the future. Accordingly, we pick stocks that we understand will appreciate and sell the ones that will depreciate.

> *"There were two sets of rules when it comes to money: One set of rules for the people who work for money and another set of rules for the rich who print money." – Robert Kiyosaki*

There are three fundamental assumptions in the technical analysis of stocks.

MARKET PRICES REFLECT ALL THE INFORMATION ABOUT A STOCK

As technical analysts, we believe that all major investors are aware of everything that they need to know about stock and company. This leads to heavy buy/sell decisions which get reflected in the market.

This information subsequently gets reflected in the stock's price and ultimately the stock chart. This is why some investors and traders only study chart patterns to gauge market trends.

STOCK PRICES FOLLOW TRENDS

Technical analysis of stocks is based on the idea that each stock chart has its own trend. Prices move only within this trend. Every move in the stock price will indicate the next move and a particular trend may or may not continue after some time.

PATTERNS TEND TO REPEAT THEMSELVES

The last assumption that validates a technical analysis is that trends are repetitive. In other words, suppose a stock chart moves in a hypothetical pattern- 1-2-3. So, each time we reach '3', we will again start from '1', and then go to '2' and eventually '3". This pattern will repeat itself without fail.

With this adhoc assumption, we can predict future stock prices based on technical analysis.

"The rich invest in time, the poor invest in money." – Warren Buffett

Based on these assumptions, we can use three important technical indicators to identify market trends and predict future stock prices.

They are

CHARTS

Price and volume charts are the most typical tools that are used as technical indicators for technical analysis. A volume chart depicts the number of shares of a company that were bought and sold in the market during a day.

Trend lines indicate the direction of movement of a stock over a period of time. We will discuss them later.

MOMENTUM INDICATORS

Momentum indicators are statistical figures that are calculated based on price and volume data of stocks. These technical indicators act as supporting tools to charts and moving averages.

Once we are through with forming an opinion about a stock based on the other tools we have discussed, we can use these indicators to confirm our views. Some momentum indicators are signs that occur before the price move we expected occurs. They confirm that the price is indeed going to move as we thought it would.

These are called leading indicators. Other signs come after the stock has started moving in a particular direction. They

"The philosophy of the rich and the poor is this: the rich invest their money and spend what is left. The poor spend their money and invest what is left." – Rich Dad

are called lagging indicators. They confirm that the stock will continue moving in this direction. Indicators are also used together with moving averages.

For example, when a stock price moves in such a way that it starts falling within a moving average, it is a confirmatory sign that it will continue to move as expected. This is called a crossover. Other popular momentum indicators include moving average convergence divergence (MACD), accumulation/distribution line.

MOVING AVERAGES

Moving averages are calculated to remove sharp, frequent fluctuations in a stock chart. Sometimes, stock prices can move very sharply in a small period of time.

This makes it hard to discover a trend in the stock chart. To remove the impact of this, and make a trend more prominent, the average of prices over a few days is calculated. For example, if a five-day pattern of a stock's price is Rs. 50, 53, 47, 45, and 52, it is difficult to tell the direction in which prices have moved. However, if we can calculate the average of these prices and compare them with the average of the next five days and the previous five days, we can ascertain a broad trend.

This kind of moving average is called a simple moving average (SMA). Other commonly used moving average concepts are exponential moving average (EMA) and linear weighted

"Although it's easy to forget sometimes, a share is not a lottery ticket. It's part ownership of a business." – Peter Lynch

average (LWA). It may be noted though, that moving averages are calculated for longer durations than five days. Ten days and one-month moving averages are more common.

IMPORTANCE OF TECHNICAL ANALYSIS

Technical analysis has gained popularity worldwide for the following reasons.

MATHEMATICAL APPROACH

Technical analysts use probability to pick stocks. By using probability, they predict the outcome of an action without necessarily needing to scrutinize it in great detail.

So, technical analysis tells us how prices are going to move without having to bother about the nitty-gritties that will cause the price to move. It is quicker and less laborious than fundamental analysis.

SIGNS OF UPCOMING DANGER

Sometimes, a major fall in stock prices is just around the corner but nobody sees it coming. Fundamental analysis tools are unable to predict it. However, by using historical chart patterns and other technical tools, one can predict the fall.

Now naturally, technical analysis cannot tell us the reason for the fall, but it can certainly tell that it is about to come. We can prepare ourselves for it accordingly.

> *"Most people give up just when they are about to achieve success. They quit on one yard line. They give up the at last minute of the game one foot from a winning touch down."* – Henry Ross Perot

For example, if a company acquires a new plant and starts producing more output from it, its revenues will go up. This should lead to an increase in its stock price. But how can we predict such a change by simply studying past charts and trends? In the short run, however, fundamental factors can only have a small effect on prices. For example, the plant we just talked about cannot start producing overnight. It will take time. In such cases, the technical analysis presents a clearer picture. Thus, technical analysis is more relevant if we want to make a quick buck in say three to six months, or even three.

Fundamental Analysis Vs. Technical Analysis

Fundamental analysis is more relevant for investors who want to invest for a long period of say three to five years or more. This is because any profitable business model takes time to be successful.

This is not so with technical analysis. Eventually, the success of a stock depends on the company's profitability. This cannot be predicted by technical analysis. It can only tell us whether the stock is going to move up or down in the near future.

Technical analysis uses past data of a stock to predict future price movements. Fundamental analysis, instead, looks at the economic and financial factors that influence a business.

"I think you have to learn that there's a company behind every stock and there's only one real reason why stocks go up. Companies go from doing poorly to doing well or small companies grow to large companies." – Peter Lynch

The first step to technical analysis starts with charts, whereas the fundamental analysis starts with the company's financial statements.

In fundamental analysis, we will have to determine a company's intrinsic value by looking at its income statement, balance sheet and cash flow statement, and other different ratios and comparing it with the peer companies. The intrinsic value of a stock can be determined by discounting the value of future projected cash flows to the net present value. If the stock trades below the company's intrinsic value, we can plan to invest in it.

But, technical analysts believe that a stock's price already reflects everything that has or could affect a company.

The time horizon in fundamental analysis is often long-term, as opposed to a short-term approach taken by technical analysis. In technical analysis stock charts can be delimited into weeks, days, or even minutes.

Technical analysts and fundamental analysts have very different goals in their minds. Technical analysis will demand that we identify many short to medium-term trades wherein we can earn a profit, whereas fundamental analysis demands us to make long-term investments.

Technical Analysis gives us an idea of time to buy and sell whereas fundamental analysis gives us an idea of whether to buy or not.

"The whole secret to winning and losing in the stock market is to lose the least amount possible when you're not right." – William J. O'Neil

The technical-analysis approach to the study of stock charts is the opposite of the fundamental approach. If we were a fundamental analyst, we would study a company's financial statements, such as the income statement and the balance sheet, to ascertain its growth potential. We would also try to monitor factors outside these financial statements that would increase the company's earnings in the future. For example, we would keep track of the new businesses the company is investing in, the new markets it is entering, and the new technology it has adopted, and so on.

Technical analysis doesn't believe in this approach. It believes that stock prices move in circles. If we can spot the section of the circle the price is currently in, we will be able to make sound investment decisions. To identify the current stage of the price pattern, we would use some analytical tools. These include various types of stock charts, some momentum indicators, and moving averages.

Diversification

Never put all your eggs in one basket. This is the central thesis on which the essence of diversification lies. If we invest all our money in one company and if the company goes bankrupt, then we shall lose all money invested. Instead of investing in one company, if we split the investment into two companies, we will reduce the odds of losing our money by, say 50%. Risks

"Volatility is greatest at turning points, diminishing as a new trend becomes established." – George Soros

and returns are directly related. Different types of assets have different risk and return characteristics. Through diversification, we will be able to balance risk and return to achieve the desired results for our financial goals. As such, diversification is one of the most important aspects, if not the most important aspect of financial planning and portfolio management.

There are two kinds of risk in Stock investments, Systematic Risk or Market Risk and Unsystematic Risk. Market risk is caused by events that affect the whole economy of the country or world. Market risk is uncontrollable and investors should be prepared for market risk when investing in Stock. The risk of the share price of a company falling due to poor financial performance or any unfavorable development which can affect the industrial sector is known as unsystematic risk. Unsystematic risk can be caused by a company or sector-specific factors. Unsystematic risk can be diversified by investing in a portfolio of stocks. If we invest in a sufficiently large number of stocks, then even if one or two stocks give poor results, our exposure to them is limited and our overall portfolio can still generate potential returns for us.

Following are some of the benefits of portfolio diversification that helps in reducing investment risk:

- **Reduces the impact of market volatility**
- **Helps achieve long-term investment plans**
- **Helps keep the capital safe**
- **Offers peace of mind**

"Time is your friend: Impulse is your enemy." – Jack Bogle

Reduces the impact of market volatility

A diversified portfolio minimizes the overall risk associated with the portfolio. Since investment is made across different asset classes and sectors, the overall impact of market volatility comes down. Owning investments across different sectors ensures that industry-specific and enterprise-specific risks are low. Thus, it reduces risks and generates higher returns in the long run.

Helps achieve long-term investment plans

The investor needs to invest in different high-performing sectors. If the market volatility has a positive impact on stocks, the investor will be able to generate higher returns on them.

Helps keep the capital safe

Not every investor is ready to play a risky game. Investors who are on the verge of retirement or have just started investing prefer stability in their portfolio and diversification ensures the protection of their savings. Diversification allows investors to achieve their investment plans while maintaining the investment risk at a minimum. It is also a method of playing safe in the volatile market.

Offers peace of mind

The biggest advantage of diversification is peace of mind. When the total investment is divided amongst a number of

---

"If you have trouble imagining a 20% loss in the stock market, you shouldn't be in stocks." – Jack Bogle

Stock, an investor will not be stressed about the performance of any particular stock in the portfolio.

Picking the Front Runners - Growth Stocks and Value Stocks

Growth Stocks and Value Stocks

Growth Stocks

Growth stocks are stocks that come with a substantially higher growth rate compared to the mean growth rate prevailing in the market. It means that the stock grows at a faster rate than the average stock in the market, consequently generating earnings at a faster rate.

Growth stocks are usually up-coming companies. Such companies usually introduce something new and innovative to the market and are growing increasingly, owing to their unique selling proposition (USP) and competitive advantage.

Growth stocks usually pay very little or no dividend at all. It is because such companies usually follow a reinvestment protocol wherein they reinvest all their retained earnings back into the company.

Growth stocks are associated with high-quality, successful companies whose earnings are expected to continue growing at an above-average rate relative to the market. Growth stocks generally have high price-to-earnings (P/E) ratios and high price-to-book ratios. The open market often places a high

"The greatest enemy of a good plan is the dream of a perfect plan. Stick to the good plan." – Jack Bogle

value on growth stocks; therefore, growth stock investors may also consider these stocks as having great worth and may be willing to pay more to own shares.

Investors who purchase growth stocks receive returns from future capital appreciation rather than dividends. Although dividends are sometimes paid to shareholders of growth stocks, it has historically been more common for growth companies to reinvest retained earnings in capital projects.

Value Stocks

Value stocks are stocks that are being traded at a value lower than their intrinsic value. It means that such stocks are undervalued. Undervalued stocks are traded at a price lower than their true value.

Value stocks are usually large, well-established companies that are undervalued for a variety of reasons, such as negative news, a bad earnings season, and so on, but eventually gain back value in the long term. Value stocks usually pay dividends well and don't reinvest the retained earnings entirely back into the company.

Value stocks generally have good fundamentals, but they may have fallen out of favor in the market and are considered bargain priced compared with their competitors. They may have prices that are below the stocks' historic levels or may be associated with new companies that aren't recognized by investors. It's possible that these companies have been affected

"An investment in knowledge pays the best interest." – Benjamin Franklin

by a problem which it may overcome soon and regain its value in the market.

Value stocks generally have a low PE ratio and low price-to-book ratio. Investors buy these stocks in the hope that there will be increase in value when the broader market recognizes their full potential, which should result in rising share prices. Thus, investors hope that if they buy these stocks at bargain prices and the stocks eventually increase in value, they could potentially make more money than if they had invested in higher-priced stocks that increased modestly in value.

Regardless of which type of investor we are, there may be a place for both growth and value stocks in our portfolio. This strategy may help us manage risk and potentially enhance our returns over time.

The decision to invest in growth vs. value stocks is ultimately left to an individual investor's preference, as well as their personal risk tolerance, investment goals, and time horizon. It should be noted that over shorter periods, the performance of either growth or value will largely depend on the point in the cycle that the market happens to be in.

Fund Allocation

So after completion of Fundamental Analysis, Technical Analysis, Diversification of Equities, and deciding on the Value and Growth Equities, we have to decide which equities can be bought from the available fund.

"If you want to be rich, simply serve more people." – *Robert Kiyosaki*

Also, how the fund is to be allocated so that in case of a major market fall or crash, the invested capital can be protected. Not only that the capital can be protected, but also the opportunity can be grabbed once the market or any Stock starts picking up.

Fund allocation for Stock buying is also as important as all the effort required to select the right Stock.

Allocation of a fund can be decided based on

Industry Sector

We have gone in detail about different sectors and their performance. We need to allocate our fund more to the sectors which are high performing like, IT, Pharma, Banking, Finance and not in less performing sectors like Paper, Hotels, Realty, Oil and Gas and others.

Growth Stock

As explained, the growth stock provides higher returns and has high risk associated. Certain percentge of fund allocation is to be allocated for growth stocks also. Investors who would like to get higher returns can allocate higher percentage of fund to growth stock.

"Value investing is simple to understand but difficult to implement. Value investors are not super sophisticated analytical wizards who create and apply intricate computer models to find attractive opportunities or assess underlying value. The hard part is discipline, patience, and judgment. Investors need discipline to avoid the many unattractive pitches that are thrown, patience to wait for the right pitch, and judgment to know when it is time to swing." – Seth Klarman

Value Stock

As explained, the value stock provides moderate returns and has low risk assoctaed. Certain percentge of fund allocation is to be allocated for value stocks also. Investors who would like to invest safe with expectation of moderate return on investment can allocate certain percentage of fund to value stock.

Market Indices Position

Market position is also and important parameter to decide on the fund to be invested in the market. If the market is at the peak, it is generally suggested to allocate less fund and wait for the market for possible correction. Allocation 100% of fund for investement in the stock market when it is at the peak is not suggested. Similarly allocation of major fund to a stock when it is at its peaks is also not recommended and suggested. Market position or Stock position is and important parmater to decide on the fund to be allocated for investment.

Risk Mitigation Strategy and Plan

An investor must consider the risk management startegy before the fund allocation. There is always the risk factor associated even we select the best of the performing sectors and value stocks. There has to be provision for fund to manage and mitigate the risk in case of market crash or any sudden fall of the stock in the bearish market. Based on the individuals Risk Management Strategy and Plan, fund is also to be allocated for managing the risk assocaited with the stock market.

"Some people get rich studying artificial intelligence. Me, I make money studying natural stupidity." – Carl Icahn

3.3 Portfolio Building

Portfolio Creation

There are four major steps to Portfolio creation:

1. Shortlisting of stocks based on Strong Fundamental
2. Shortlisting of Stocks based on Technical Analysis
3. Diversification of Portfolio
4. Fund Allocation

"Big companies have small moves, small companies have big moves."
– Peter Lynch,

Shortlisting of Stocks based on Strong Fundamentals

Shortlisting of Equities based on strong fundamentals is the most important step and one needs to spend considerable time to narrow down to good equities that would give good returns in the future.

Fundamental analysis is usually done to find the intrinsic value of a stock.

Fundamental analysis is not just about quantitative valuations but also intangible factors like management quality, corporate governance standards, and disclosure levels. When we study its intangible factors and quantitative valuation, we come to know about the fundamentals and find a reasonable benchmark to value the companies.

When we look into the quantitative valuation of the company, we look for growth in sales, profit, and margin and the different ratios and parameters of the company as listed below.

1. P/E ratio	To be compared with sector PE
2. Price-to-book value	Preferred lower as compared to peer companies in the same industry.
3. Debt-to-Stock ratio	Preferred less than 1.
4. Operating profit margin	The higher ratio is preferred but depends on the on sector.
6. Return on Stock	Higher the better

"It's far better to buy a wonderful company at a fair price, than a fair company at a wonderful price." – Warren Buffett

7. Interest coverage ratio	Higher the better.
8. Current ratio	Preferred more than 1
9. Asset turnover ratio	Higher the better
10. Dividend yield	Higher the better

Intangibles factors like management quality, corporate governance standards, and the disclosure levels are also very important and give an idea of how efficiently the company is being run and how it is rewarding the capital and investments.

The company's ability to manage its uniqueness in the market for its quality, monopoly, service level, cost-effectiveness, etc. are very important to decide on the fundamentals.

Fundamentally strong companies can sustain through the worst of times.

Based on the Quantitative and Qualitative analysis we shortlist the companies with strong fundamentals which have to be diversified and should also have value and growth stocks.

Shortlisting of Stocks based on Technical Analysis

Once we are done with fundamental Analysis and shortlisted the stocks, we do the Technical Analysis where we mainly focus on finding the trend of the stock. Upward Trend is the friend of investors so we have narrow it down to the stocks which are in the upward trend.

"If a business does well, the stock eventually follows." – Warren Buffett

Technical analysis use price charts and tells us the direction of the security i.e., stock, index, currency, or commodity. Along with direction, we also get an idea about entry and exit prices.

Technical analysis helps forecast the direction of prices. This is done through the study of past market data, like price and volume. Price is the rate at which the security traded at different points in time. Volume is the number of trades that were done.

Analysis of the chart can be based on weekly, 3 months, 6 months, and yearly data to find its trend.

We look for:

> Upward Trend to buy a stock for investment.
>
> Downward Trend to look for the stock we already have to decide to sell or hold.
>
> Sideways Trend to decide to buy or sell or hold.

Based on our findings we decide and narrow down our list further which was prepared after completion of fundamental analysis to quality for buying.

Diversification

The list finalized after the technical analysis is now checked for diversification.

"Only buy something that you'd be perfectly happy to hold if the market shut down for 10 years." – Warren Buffett

The diversification can be based on individual choices but the following rule can be taken up to understand the diversification.

Categorize the Stocks into the Value Equities

Categorize the Stocks into Growth Equities

Categorize the Stock sectors into Declining, Stable, Growing, Future based on the market scenario and give weightage

Fund Allocation

Allocate the fund to each sector and to the Stock based on the Price and Quantity to be procured. It is necessary to keep some fund available as contingency fund that can be utilized for cost averaging when required and for other risks accociated with the market.

"To a value investor, investments come in three varieties: undervalued at one price, fairly valued at another price, and overvalued at still some higher price. The goal is to buy the first, avoid the second, and sell the third." – Seth Klarman

3.4 Winning Strategies for Working Professionals

For working professionals, major challenge is time and hence any investment made in the stock market should be safe even if much time is not devoted to the stock market on account of the time required for active source of earning i.e the job. Hence it is required to have investment is right Stocks to ensure no capital erosion and gain in most of the stocks. Also the strategy should give consistent and regular growth on the investment from the market. Continuous gain of knowledge

"Once you find the system that works for your style/personality and confidence is gained, wash, rinse, repeat over and over again."

on Stock Market is always an added advantage over and above return on investment.

Below are some of major investing winning strategies that can followed by working professionals based on their personality traits

- **Minimum Risk Regular Return Investment Strategy**
- **Buying Cheap and Selling Dear Strategy**
- **Rupee Cost Averaging Strategy**
- **Buying at Target and Selling at Target Strategy**
- **Momentum Algotrading Investment Strategy**
- **Periodic Fusion Investment Strategy**
- **5/10/15 Year Maturity Investment Plan**
- **Lump Sum Investing**

Minimum Risk Regular Return Investment Strategy

This strategy considers the following basic points of investment and profit making.

Invest Regularly

Book Profit Regularly

Diversify your investment in different Sectors

"All you need is one pattern to make a living." – Linda Raschke

Planning and Execution for Investment

    Diversify your investment within Sectors

    Invest in sectors which are performing

    Accept that some of the investment may take considerable time to give return

    Accept that some of the investment may sink and there may be complete erosion of capital invested in few of the stocks.

    Assume and Accept Profit Booking in the Range of 15 to 30 % on major portion (upto 70 %) of the investment, higher than 30% on minor portion (upto 25 %) of the investments and poor, no return or loss on meager portion (upto 5%) of the investment.

Selection of only fundamentally strong Stocks are to be done with right Entry and Exit Strategy in place.

This strategy can also be compared with the business model of an apparel store.

Let us see how business works for a profitable apparel store in a local market and make a strategy for investment in stock market based on this Business Model.

This needs:

1. A large variety inventory which meets the choices of customers

---

"The core problem, however, is the need to fit markets into a style of trading rather than finding ways to trade that fit with market behavior." – Brett Steenbarger

In General an Apparel Store has large inventory which can meet the choices of its customers. But almost all items need to be of good quality and need to be updated with the ongoing trend and fashion.

Similarly our portfolio should have Quality and Diversified Stocks which are fundamentally strong. This is not a difficult task as there are many good performing companies in most of the sectors which provides good return on investment and dividend. We need to identify such stocks and buy them at right point in time based on the technical study on the stock and market condition.

Summary: Get your portfolio diversified with fundamentally strong companies. This will help to manage the risks associated with stock market and also help to generate regular and consistent profit.

2. Inventory with Recent Trend and fashion

   An Apparel Store keeps most up-to-date and recently trending stuff so that there is regular visit of the customers for the items in fashion and also higher profit can booked by selling the items in trend and fashion.

   In Stock Market, sectors represent what is in fashion. There are some of the sectors which are high performing during a certain period of time which may

"If you can't take a small loss, sooner or later you will take the mother of all losses." – Ed Seykota

be for short or long duration. Some of the stocks are available at premium price but still have potential to grow. There may be some stocks which may not be at premium now but has the potential to be a premium stock in the future. We have to identify such sectors and make our investment accordingly. We have to ensure that stocks we buy are fundamentally strong. We may hold them for some time to grow and sell at a higher price, booking higher returns on the investment.

Summary: Identify some of the sectors which are performing well and make investment accordingly. Such investment will provide higher return in short period of time.

3. High Turnover of inventory

    Apparel Stores have many fast moving items which keep the inventory rolling and provide opportunity to buy new inventory which are more up-to date and as per market demand. This also ensures regular profit booking and fund rotation.

    In Stock Market also, we have to find the stocks which can provide good return in short duration of time. The stocks which are fundamentally strong and are mostly volatile can be targeted for building portfolio. Also such stocks should be having cyclic or

---

"Amateurs think about how much money they can make. Professionals think about how much money they could lose." – Jack Schwager

upward movement. We should target to get return of 15 to 30 percent from these stocks.

Summary: Portfolio should have some stocks which can give us profit in the short term because of its volatility or its upward trend. This helps to book regular profit from the market on short term basis and helps to book profit and rotate the fund invested.

4. Slow Moving Apparel Stocks

   Apparel Stores have some stocks which are high priced and slow moving. There are few stocks which may not be high priced but are slow moving. We have to wait to get the right customer to buy such stocks, who are ready to pay the price of the stock.

   Similarly our portfolio may have some stocks which may be slow moving. Such stocks gets stuck at a price below the purchase price and do not move upwards and there is possibility of price falling further. We have to wait for selling such stocks for considerable time. Sometimes such Stocks are to be sold at loss to save the current investment value at market price.

   Summary: - All investments will not give good returns. Some of the stocks in portfolio take longer period to give return. If we get reasonable return on

"The key to trading success is emotional discipline. If intelligence were the key, there would be a lot more people making money trading... I know this will sound like a cliche, but the single most important reason that people lose money in the financial markets is that they don't cut their losses short." – Victor Sperandeo

investment of 10 – 20 % annually in such cases, we should book profit at appropriate time. Some stocks have to be sold at discount to get the capital free for investment in others better stocks.

5. Remain updated with the Upcoming Trend and Fashion

Apparel Stores have to remain updated with the upcoming Trend and Fashion and plan accordingly to try and test the related products in the local market. This helps them build the inventory at the right point in time and book high profit once the fashion is at its peak.

In Stock market also we have to keep searching the growth stock and sectors which can do exceptionally well. It is suggested to identify and make small investments in such growth stocks. Also it is suggested to make a list of such growth stocks and monitor them on continuous basis for their movement and invest accordingly.

Summary: - Investment in growth stocks gives very good return and hence needs continuous research, analysis and monitoring. It takes time to identify such stock and once invested we have to remain invested for getting outstanding return from the investment. Also investment in such stocks have to be increased at regular interval to get better return.

"Bull markets are born on pessimism, grow on skepticism, mature on optimism and die of euphoria." – John Templeton

Similarly, upcoming and emerging technologies may completely change the investment pattern and few sectors may get benefited from the new and emerging technology. Research and development in Cloud Services, Internet Of Things, Industrial Internet of Things, Artificial Intelligence, Machine Leaning, Blockchain, Crypto currency, Connected Smart Homes, Mega-constellations of satellites, Low-earth orbit satellite systems, Autonomous Cars and Vehicles, Quantum Computing, Human Augmentations and Nanorobotics may bring drastic changes to many sectors and accordingly the stock market will dance to the tune of major technological changes expected in future.

6. Get Rid of Old and Out of Fashion Stock through Sale

Apparel Stores in Malls and in local market offer sale of products where items are sold at a lower price with different schemes. The goal is to generate revenue and get rid of old and out of fashion stock.

In Stock market also, we may come across some bad investments and we have to plan to get rid of such stocks by selling them at a discount. Strategy is to be made and implemented so that we get out of such bad investment.

Summary: - There may be some bad investments. It is suggested to get out of such investments as soon

"Only when the tide goes out do you discover who's been swimming naked." – Warren Buffett

as possible. Losses in stock market is inevitable and some of the investments will go wrong. Corrective measure is to be taken by selling them.

Sometimes it is possible to average out the cost for such investments and come out with profit booking, but the decision to average out the cost is risky and hence is to be thought upon well before making further investment.

7. Small Inventory and Just in Time Approach

   Apparel Stores follow the small inventory per item so that available fund can be utilized for buying more products to meet customers' demands of different varieties. They also follow just in time approach to maintain minimum inventory.

   In Stock Market too, making 1st investment low on most of the stock works well as it saves from sudden fall in the stock market or sudden fall in the price of the stock purchased. Since the 1st Investment on any particular stock is less, the losses are also less and it can be managed by cost averaging out at right point in time. If the price starts appreciating, the inventory can be built to get maximum return from the investment.

   Summary: - Making the 1st Investment low in the stock market saves us from many uncertainties and

"I make no attempt to forecast the market—my efforts are devoted to finding undervalued securities." – Warren Buffett

risks of the stock market. Also this gives opportunity to diversify as the fund is available to buy other good and quality stocks.

Minimum Risk Regular Return Investment Strategy (Apparel Store Investment Strategy) aptly suits working professionals as the risk of investment in stock market is mitigated and managed to a great extent by diversification in the investment. It also gives opportunity to gain knowledge on the market and stocks. It is suggested not to make lots of transactions for every investment/stocks rather we have to give time to get the stocks for providing good returns. Making no activity for some time at regular intervals gives very good return on this strategy. This strategy also helps to take advantage of value stocks, growth stocks, volatility of the stocks. It also helps to take advantage of stocks with falling prices which gives good return if remain invested. So the major risk of bear market of which every working professional is scared of is taken care and also it turns in favour as profit. The key to this strategy is that the investment in only the fundamentally strong stocks are to be selected. Timing of entry and Exit in any stock is as important as in any strategy.

"A market downturn doesn't bother us. It is an opportunity to increase our ownership of great companies with great management at good prices." – Warren Buffett

Buying Cheap and Selling Dear Strategy

The real challenge for many investors is that, they notice and get interested in certain stocks when there is a run-up. They generally invest at high levels of markets and find it difficult to book profits on such investments.

A price-to-earnings (P/E) ratio based investment approach works better for them as it keeps emotions away.

In this Strategy we look for the intrinsic value of the stock and find out some fundamentally strong stocks with low PE as compared to sector PE. We also look for the trend of the stock and buy when the prices are lower and rising trend has been established. Once the stock price increase and we get the desired return we can sell the stock. Also we can use training stop loss to ensure maximum return from the trend established.

Buying Cheap and Selling Dear is also one of the most commonly used strategies for short term investment and for getting good return on investment.

This strategy demands time to do some research on the stocks so that right stock can be picked for investment.

Other factors like fundamentally strong company, technical study, trend, sector performance etc. are also to be considered before making investment.

"You only have to do a very few things right in your life so long as you don't do too many things wrong." – Warren Buffett

Rupee Cost Averaging Strategy

Rupee Cost Averaging (RCAS) is a very common plan of investment which works very well for working professionals for long term investment. Investors can invest small amount at regular or at different intervals based on market conditions and get the benefit of rupee cost averaging and power of compounding together enabling us to build wealth over time.

The RCAS route is the preferred way of investing in stocks market because it allows us to participate in the market with small investment while managing risk better.

Advantages of RCAS

Price averaging: RCAS allows us to average out the price over a long period so that the impact of fluctuating prices of stock market is minimized. We can buy more quantity of stocks when the prices drop and buy less when the prices go up.

The advantage is that we need not bother about market fluctuations and needn't even time the market either.

Discipline: RCAS instils a sense of discipline towards investment and savings. Hence RCAS is to be done regularly. When the prices are high, less Qty is to be purchased and when the price falls, more Qty is to be purchased. This ensures we acquire the asset at a lower average cost.

"Compound interest is the eighth wonder of the world. He who understands it, earns it. He who doesn't, pays it." – Albert Einstein

Regular investment helps to make a big fund in the long run.

Low initial Investment: We can start RCAS with a much lower amount compared to other investments.

Flexibility of Investment: RCAS provides flexibility in investment. Based on our fund availability and Market Price of the stock, we can plan for investment.

Lower risk: Lump sum investments may expose us to a greater capital risk. RCAS spreads our investment over time and reduces the risk to capital and helps us navigate volatility better.

Buying at Target and Selling at Target

This strategy of Investment uses target to buy and sell.

This works well for working professionals as the target of buying and selling is fixed based on the return expected.

The target for buying any stock can be decided like, 3 Years average Price, 12 months low from Current Market Price, 25 % low from the current Market Price etc. based on the individuals choice.

Similarly Target for selling is decided like 25 % high from the purchase price.

Investors can set the Target for buying and Selling in the system and system executes the order once the target set is achieved.

"Beware the investment activity that produces applause; the great moves are usually greeted by yawns." – Warren Buffett

This really helps working professionals as a lot of time is saved.

As mentioned above, other factors like fundamentally strong company, technical study, trend, sector performance etc hold good and are also to be considered before making investment through this strategy.

Algotrading helps to achieve this strategy very well. So this strategy can be executed with help of algotrading which will minimize the effort in stock selection, monitoring the stocks etc

Also the feature of training stop loss of algotrading will help to maximize the profit if we do not set the target for sale for stocks.

Momentum Algorithmic Trading Investment Strategy

Momentum Algorithmic trading can be highly beneficial for the investors who wants to invest large amount and are planning for a short term investment and return in the range of few days to few weeks. In Momentum Algorithmic trading investors can set the criteria for selection and executions of orders automatically.

It uses automated program to follow a defined set of instructions for placing a trade in order to generate profits at a high speed and frequency that is practically not possible for a human. Also program/codes is used to analyze the data and chart to enter and exit trades according to set parameters such as price movements, volatility levels, and volume etc. Once the current

"The most important quality for an investor is temperament, not intellect." – Warren Buffett

market conditions match any predetermined criteria, trading algorithms can execute a buy or sell order on someone's behalf. This saves times on continuously monitoring the market and timing the trade.

Because of its automated logic based capabilities on many parameters and executions, it can be of great help to retail investors and working professionals who want their fund to rotate fast and get higher returns.

Apart from profit opportunities for the trader, algorithmic - trading provides more systematic way of trading and investing by ruling out the impact of human emotions and other human behaviors which impact the decisions in stock Market.

Investors and Traders can provide different instructions in algorithmic trading and the instructions will be executed as order once the criteria are met. The need to regularly monitoring the trade, live process and graph of stocks is reduced to minimum when using algorithmic trading.

Algorithmic - trading provides many benefits and following are few:

- Execute multiple orders & portfolios simultaneously
- Provides Automation of Process for entry and exit positions
- Can manage both, buy-side and sell-side trades across different class of assets including spot market and derivative.

"It is impossible to produce superior performance unless you do something different from the majority." – John Templeton

- Reduced the possibility of mistakes by human traders based on emotional and psychological factors.
- Trades are executed at the best possible prices as planned and instructed
- It can fine tune the risk management in our trading strategy, implementing stops and limits on our behalf.
- Trade order placement is instant. (There is a high chance of execution at the desired levels).
- Trades are timed correctly and instantly to avoid significant price changes.
- Reduced transaction costs.
- Simultaneous automated checks on multiple market conditions.
- Reduced risk of manual errors when placing trades.
- Set your algorithms up anytime 24 x 7 and let it trade on your behalf.
- Helps in trend identification, scalping, position sizing, stop loss trailing
- Convenience, Speed, Flexibility, Reliability and Access from anywhere and any device.

Also, it provides support on selecting the right stock based on different filters required to select the desired stock. It is impossible for an investor to analyze large chunks of data and

"The men who have succeeded are men who have chosen one line and stuck to it." – Andrew Carnegie

act on it within a short period of time which can be otherwise be easily handled by algorithmic trading.

Algorithmic trading has been gaining traction with both retail and institutional traders. It is widely used by investment banks, pension funds, mutual funds, and hedge funds. A study in 2019 reveals that that more than 90% of trading in the Forex market was performed by trading algorithms.

With momentum algorithmic trading strategy all the investment criteria can be defined right from the stock selection to the order execution for sale. User also gets input from the system to buy and sell a particular stock based on the technical analysis and chart.

This strategy provides lots of flexibility to decide and adopt your own criteria for investment and also in making the necessary changes to maximize the profit and return from the investment.

PFIS:- Periodic Fusion Investment Strategy

Periodic Fusion Investment Strategy is another investment Strategy where investment is to be done periodically (quarterly, half yearly, annually) in both, value and growth stocks by the working professionals for the variables, bonuses, allowance and other handout pay they receive at regular intervals.

"The best way to measure your investing success is not by whether you're beating the market but by whether you've put in place a financial plan and a behavioral discipline that are likely to get you where you want to go." – Benjamin Graham

Since this is not a regular investment, a fusion of growth and value stock can be chosen to build the portfolio with certain percentage allocated to both kinds of stock.

This strategy makes a balanced investment and risk associated with the stock market is taken care. Also high return from the growth stock can be availed. Selected Value Stocks also provides good dividend and steady growth of the fund invested.

A portfolio with fusion of Value and Growth Stocks is a good option for many working professional as they invest half quarterly, half yearly or annually.

This strategy needs market and stock study to a great extent so that right stock can be selected for long term investment. Since some of the Growth stock may or may not perform as expected, course correction will be needed and based on the performance of growth stocks, their early sale and exit can also be planned.

This is a long term investment strategy where associated risk can be managed with diversification and cost averaging. Portfolio Building in this strategy has to be done very carefully after enough research on the stock. Regular monitoring of Growth Stock is also required for their performance and continuance in the portfolio.

"Calling someone who trades actively in the market an investor is like calling someone who repeatedly engages in one-night stands a romantic." – Warren Buffett

5/10/15 Year Progressive Maturity Investment Strategy or Systematic Withdrawal Strategy (SWS)

5/10/15 Year Maturity Progressive Investment Strategy is the investment strategy in which investment is initiated on rupee cost averaging strategy for a one year and the investment along with return from the market may be withdrawn at the start of 6th Year. This can also be considered as systematic withdrawal Strategy (SWS).

So every year a new stock is selected and investment is made on rupee cost averaging strategy for a year so that every next year (6th Year onwards) a hefty grown up sum is available for usage/investment.

This investment strategy ensures

- Regular investment
- Regular withdrawal of investment sum and profit 5th years onwards

This is also a long term investment strategy where associated risk can be managed with diversification and cost averaging. Portfolio Building in this strategy has to be done very carefully after enough research on the stock. Regular monitoring of Growth Stock is also required for their performance and continuance in the portfolio.

"The stock market is designed to transfer money from the active to the patient." – Warren Buffett

This strategy of investment can be started at an early age by working professionals who like to get back the returns along with investment at a regular interval after certain time period.

Lump - Sum Investing Strategy

Lump-sum Investing Strategy is one of the very simple strategy and gives very good return if remain invested for considerably longer duration like 15 to 35 years.

The stock section is key is such investment and diversification to an extent is also suggested in lump sum investment.

In this strategy, we invest only once in selected stocks and then wait for considerable time to get very good return from the investment.

This is a hassle free strategy which saves time and can be used to park and grow the surplus fund that is available with someone.

Investment with diversification and combination of Growth and Value Stock in building the right portfolio will help to get better profit and also to mitigate the risks.

This strategy needs proper study of the stocks before investment can be done. Enough time has to be given for portfolio building through this investment strategy.

Let us see some examples on the returns of some of the investments.

"If you aren't thinking about owning a stock for 10 years, don't even think about owning it for 10 minutes." – Warren Buffett

Planning and Execution for Investment

Investment - 1 Lakh								Value - In Lakh	
	5 Years Before		10 Years Before		15 Years Before		20 Years Before		Data - Mar 2021
	Value	%age Return	Value	%age Return	Value	%age Return	Value	%age Return	
Bajaj Finance Ltd	7.71	671	76	7505	109	10865	345	34480	
Pidilite Ind	3.08	208	12.48	1148	34.76	3376	84	8307	
Asian Paints	2.93	193	9.95	896	39.74	3874	65	6396	
Balkrishna Ind	5.35	435	24.7	2370	19.38	18.39	61	6069	
Kotak Mahindra Bank	2.69	169	7.9	690	25.64	2464	53.1	5210	
Britannia Ind.	2.74	174	19.75	1875	19.61	1861	41.67	4067	
HDFC Bank	2.8	181	6.21	521	17.67	1667	26.93	2593	

Mentioned below are key points that one needs to consider while investing along with the investment strategies described above. Key points mentioned below apply to all the strategies of investment.

Portfolio Building Takes Time

Building a sound portfolio takes time. It requires patience and adherence on the part of the investor.

When we give sufficient time for portfolio building, we can take all possible right steps and mitigate all possible risks involved like market conditions, economic situations, high investment by FII, DII, and other factors.

As **Warren Buffet** famously said, "The stock market is designed to transfer money from the impatient to the patient." An investor needs to give time to his stocks to compound over the period.

Look for Value and Invest in Future

We need to know the current value and the value to be created for a Stock.

Value creation is related to prospects of the company, sustainability of its products or services, the ability to generate capital to meet future demand, and its ability to implement

> *"I never attempt to make money on the stock market. I buy on the assumption that they could close the market the next day and not reopen it for five years." – Warren Buffett*

technological innovations. The growth of a stock depends on its earning capacity to generate demand for its product/services and the company's ability to execute it. This approach requires thorough research and understanding of the business on the part of investors.

While devising a plan for investment, it is imperative to understand where the investment is being made and whether it is worth investing.

The market is always future-oriented. Nokia which enjoyed the market leader position couldn't capture the smartphone wave and ultimately lost to technically superior companies like Samsung, Apple, and others. Indian wrist watch maker HMT lost the ground as it could not upgrade its product with time and per customer requirements.

A value company will ride through these challenges and keep customers glued to their products.

Plan, Analyze, and Conclude

Prediction about the market does not work most of the time. To become a successful investor, it is crucial to first plan the investment. Based on the plan, one must analyze the structure of the market and the company one plans to invest in. Analyzing trade or investment includes studying the stock records, technical analysis of patterns, and the time to buy or

"Should you find yourself in a chronically leaking boat, energy devoted to changing vessels is likely to be a more productive than energy devoted to patching leaks." – Warren Buffett

sell. Once an individual gets a hang of all these aspects of the market, they are ready to execute their investment plan.

Therefore, do the homework properly before investing. We should only invest in what we know and devote time to learn about what we don't know.

Avoid The Rush and Crowd

We need not invest in a particular stock simply because people around us are investing in it. This may not yield good returns and one may end up with heavy losses in the long run.

We need to invest only where we see value even at the cost of missing some known major moves.

Diversification is the Key

Diversification is the key to success in the stock market if we are investing in Stocks for good returns. Investment in Stock Market carries risk as some of the companies we invest in can underperform, or even wind up entirely. But if we diversify our portfolio, we will be safeguarding against losing our assets when investments don't go as planned.

Diversifying a portfolio across asset classes can help us earn optimum returns with minimum risk. The kind and level of diversification can vary from investor to investor, and it can help cope up with volatility, something that is part and parcel of the stock market.

> *"The most important thing to do if you find yourself in a hole is to stop digging." – Warren Buffett*

It is always advisable to diversify a portfolio across asset classes, as it can help minimize risks.

Diversification is key to get good return from the stock market and to manage the risk. Hence diversification is picked as a topic to explain many a times in the book at different places.

Follow the Discipline

It is always prudent to invest systematically and with patience in the right shares or funds. As the stock market is always volatile, an investor should be ready to absorb calculated risk and decide a necessary course of action like hedging against underlying stocks. **Discipline is the key to success.**

Have Realistic Expectations on Returns

It is crucial to have realistic expectations from the market on the expected returns. The Stock market tends to deliver returns at its own pace. It is known to test an investor's patience all the time. Therefore, we have to look for the opportunity it gives to earn money and high return, rather than timing it at our end and expecting the result to come as per our expectation.

In fact, no asset-class can give abnormally high returns for a long time and the Stock market is no exception to this principle. Unrealistic expectations always leads to disappointment and wrong investment decisions which eventually turn out to be a lost game.

"Investing should be more like watching paint dry or watching grass grow. If you want excitement, take $800 and go to Las Vegas."
– Paul Samuelson

Invest only Surplus Funds

An investor should only invest surplus funds that they don't need in the short run, or in a medium span of time. Since the Stock market is volatile, there is always a risk of temporary loss or locking of money in some of the investments done.

So, when we invest out surplus fund in stock market, we have the patience to wait for the expected profit. Once we diversify, we will find that some of the stocks will give a quick return, some will take moderate time and few will take a considerable long time to give the result.

The stock market moves in cycles, and it requires the right temperament to go along with it. Investment of surplus fund eases our mental makeup, thereby helping us remain invested in the market as long as required and reap the benefit at the appropriate time.

Control Emotions

Several investors lose their money in stock markets as they are not able to control their emotions. When investing in a bull market, there is a lure to invest more and more, which results in rash investments in wrong shares. Fear and greed are two factors that have to be controlled when we enter the stock market.

When prices start falling sharply, investors fear that it will fall even more and start selling in panic. Panic selling causes

"Without Strategy Execution is Aimless and without Execution strategy is useless." – Morris Chang

stock prices to fall sharply. Ultimately, prices fall to such low levels that stock valuations become attractive (cheap) and the markets eventually bottom out.

As we know, Stock prices follow the **law of demand and supply**. With the higher demand i.e. more money flowing in, the prices keep rising further and profits keep growing. Growing profits fuel more greed and more money gets invested eventually raising prices to an excessive level. At very high prices, asset bubbles are created i.e. prices are much more than the intrinsic or fundamental value of assets. Like all bubbles, asset bubbles eventually burst and prices crash drastically. Investors who had bought stocks at very high prices face big losses when the market corrects. So greed rockets up investment to an unsustainable level leading to a deep fall eroding the capital invested.

Thus, skillful control of emotion can prove to be the real differentiator when it comes to success and failure. Our mental state has a significant impact on the decisions we make, particularly if we are new to the stock market, and keeping a calm demeanor is important for making a good return and to continue in the market in the long run.

Use the Strength of Compounding

Although it's possible to make money on the stock market in the short term, the real earning potential comes from the

"We don't have to be smarter than the rest. We have to be more disciplined than the rest." – Unknown

compound interest we earn on long-term holdings. As our assets increase in value, the total amount of money in our account grows, making room for even more capital gains. That's how stock market earnings increase over time exponentially.

But to take advantage of that exponential growth, we need to start building our portfolio as early as possible. Ideally, we should start investing as soon as we start earning.

Continue to Invest Regularly from the Early Age

Time is an important component of our overall portfolio growth.

The right time to invest is from the time we start earning. By investing at an early stage of life, we learn financial independence and discipline.

If we invest early and incur a loss, we have more time to make up for the losses. Also with early age investments, we develop a habit of saving more. The more you invest, the more you reap in future. Young investors have more risk-taking ability than older ones.

Moreover early investments lead to compounding returns. The time value of money increases over a period of time. Regular investments made right from an early age can cumulate into huge benefits at the time of retirement.

Investing early allows us to develop disciplined spending habits by focusing on our budget and cutting expenses when needed.

> *"If you don't study any companies, you have the same success buying stocks as you do in a poker game if you bet without looking at your cards." – Peter Lynch*

Through early investment, the lessons learned pay off in the long run, especially when we have more capital to work with and restraint is needed.

Additionally, at some point our finances may become unstable, but by investing early remain prepared to face such hardships.

Earlier we invest, the richer we get and financial situation will be better down the line.

Get advice and guidance from Investment Professionals

Hiring the right investment and financial advisor can always help. Even though the use of a professional can't mitigate all risks of losses, we feel more comfortable knowing that there is an expert in the corner to help and advice.

Financial advisors focus on providing personalized advice on our investment portfolio, typically for a fee based on a percentage of assets under management.

Another lower-cost way to get guidance on investing is to use a Robo-advisor.

Start Small

Starting small saves us and reduces the risk to a very great extent. When we are new to the market, the best strategy is to

"Go to the mouse you foolish investor and learn. A mouse never entrusts its life to only one hole." – Ajaero Tony Martins

invest a small portion of the available money and focus on only a few stocks. The strategy is to **invest less and learn more.**

Acquire more knowledge for the slow and consistent growth of the fund.

Once we are comfortable with the stock market investment and understand the fundamentals, we can plan to invest more and big.

Penny Stocks

Penny stocks are stocks that trade at very low prices, and have low market capitalization.

These are also called nano-cap stocks, micro-cap stocks, and small-cap stocks, depending on the company's market capitalization.

These stocks (penny stocks) are lesser-known to the larger investing public as investors remain away from them because the information regarding their fundamentals and businesses is either not reliable or not available. These stocks mostly give higher returns but also can give major losses that cannot be recovered.

It is suggested to stay away from penny stocks. These stocks can get delisted from major stock exchanges also.

Penny stocks give very high profit but the chances of losing money are also high.

The above are some of the important points to be considered and taken care of when we start investing.

"Forecasting is like trying to turn lead into gold." – Philip Fisher

3.5 Common Mistakes of Investors

There is an old but very famous joke about the stock market. If you have lost some money in the stock market and feel bad about it, don't worry. Ask somebody you know about their losses in the stock market, and you would feel better, for, you lost less money.

While this joke has been doing rounds for several decades now and is still quite relevant because there is absolutely no shortage of people who lose money in stock markets every day.

"Investing is not nearly as difficult as it looks. Successful investing involves doing a few things right and avoiding serious mistakes."
– Jack Bogle

According to popular estimates, as much as 90% to 95 % of people lose their money in stock markets, and this includes both new and seasoned investors too.

There are countless reasons why investors lose money in stock markets. Let's take a detailed look at some of the top reasons.

Investing based on Rumors and Stock Tips

Have you ever received an SMS which reads like this "Buy 1000 quantity of XYZ stocks for xx price? Huge upside expected in one month as it will be acquired by ABC Company" or "Invest in bulk in XYZ stock as the company **is going** to soon acquire exclusive distribution rights of ABC product or service. Buy now at a low price of XY – Capital to sell at a high price of Capital – XYZ within a few months"?

Such messages are deliberately sent through bulk SMS by fraudsters who operate as a stock market cartel with the sole intention to cheat innocent investors by trapping them into buying stocks that have no fundamentals associated.

Many investors, especially new ones, fall for the trap of investing based on stock tips given by others.

Investing in Penny Stocks Market

Just like the name suggests, penny stocks are stocks that trade at very low prices, usually in single digits or even lower. The

"You know… you keep doing the same things and you keep getting the same result over and over again." – Warren Buffett

low cost is what makes them attractive to some investors. However, in this process, investors often forget that price and value are two different things.

Penny stocks have low market capitalization, and very little information is available about them in the public domain. They are highly susceptible to management frauds and financial mismanagement.

Not Investing in Fundamentally Sound Business

Fundamentally sound stocks have a transparent and robust business model and professionally well-managed. Such companies can survive any economic downturns and are usually the first to recover and outperform as when the economy improves.

As we might be aware of the year 2008, witnessed one of the worst corrections in the history of stock markets. Many investors panicked and sold their investments for heavy losses as if there was no tomorrow. However, those who remained invested were rewarded immensely as the market recovered in less than 24 months.

Buying the Falling Stocks

Sometimes continuous buying of falling stocks can be devastating for the investors. There can be many valid reason for the continuous fall of the price of stock and if the company

'A lot of people with high IQs are terrible investors because they've got terrible temperaments. You need to keep raw, irrational emotion under control." – Charlie Munger

gets into financial trouble and management issues which the company is not able to manage will lead to complete erosion of the capital invested. So we have to be very careful while buying the stocks which are falling. Some of falling stocks give good returns too but we have to do our homework diligently before making investment in such stocks.

Chopping the Winners

Selling the Stocks at a small profit is another mistake that most of the investors do. There are many cases where investors make small profit by selling stocks which could have given fantastic returns in due course of time and also they make huge losses by keeping the loss making and falling stocks. It's working wrong both ways for the investors.

Identifying the stocks which has the potential to grow and give good returns and remain invested is key to making good profit from stock market.

Herding/Following the crowd

Investors feel more secure by following the herd mentality especially during uncertainties in the financial market. Herding behavior in the stock market can be of the following forms.

"Unless you can watch your stock holding decline by 50% without becoming panic stricken, you should not be in the stock market."
– Warren Buffett

Reputation based: - Reputation-based herding is caused by a respected investor or major trading house taking a specific trading stance.

Compensation based: - This herding occurs when large institutional investors money managers book profits, to protect fund earnings.

Information based: - This herding happens when majority reacts the same way to announced information.

Trade Imbalance: - Whenever there is unusual large volume of trade, investors speculates for certain reason and follows herding thinking for certain event or news behind the high volume of trade.

Anchoring

Anchoring is another factor which stops investors from getting good return from the market. Anchoring makes Investors to get glued to some of the stocks or fall in love with some of them. Most of the common stocks to which most of the working professionals are glued are HDFC Bank, Axis Bank, ITC, Hindustan Unilever, Reliance Industries, Tata Motors, SBI, Tata Steel and few more similar value stocks. This makes them to miss the opportunity to invest in growth stocks which could have given them much better return. Also Anchoring leads to make some fixed mindset about some of the sectors as being non-performers and it stops them from investing in those sectors. Once such sectors

"Emotions are your worst enemy in the stock market." – Don Hays

picks up and gives good return, the opportunity is missed by investors who had made up their mind for poor performance of some sectors or stocks.

Gambling

Many a times working professionals put the money in stock market for fun and try their luck. Such event has an uncertain outcome and heavily involves chance. Also such investment turns out to be poorly planned majority of times, leading to bad experience from the stock market. The probability of losing in gambling is usually higher than the probability of winning and hence gambling is to be avoided.

Every investment in stock market has to be supported by logic, study and analysis.

Lack of Patience

Some investors lacks patience and sell loss making stocks only to realize that it would have given them good profit if they would have holded it for some more time. Same way buying in hurry can lead to buying at high.

Patience is key to success in stock market as remain invested bring good result most of the time in stock market. If our study and analysis indicate us for waiting for fall of price of a particular stock, we should wait for making investment. Buying in hurry can lead to buying at high cost.

"Only those who are asleep make no mistakes." – Ingvar Kamprad

High Turnover

High Turnover is another stumbling block for high return from Stock Market.

High Turnover on stocks can lead to eroding profit and also make liable for short term tax payment. Also it can be the opportunity cost of missing out on the long-term gains of other sensible investments.

No Stop Loss

Most of the investors do not use the Stop Loss feature and make huge losses on their investment on some of the wrong stocks purchased.

Investment done on short term are to be monitored closely and Stop Loss feature is to be utilized and used as and when needed.

Short Selling

Short Selling in spot market can be done whenever we are sure of any stock going falling. We have to be very careful in short selling as if we do not square up our positions on the same day then these stocks will automatically result in delivery.

"Reaching any goal in trading requires specific domain knowledge and technical skills. But then, after that, it's all mindset management. Yet most people ignore that —they automatically think they have that last part all figured out, and it's a mistake." – Yvan Byeajee,

Short selling in futures is a better option than short selling in spot market as selling in the cash market runs the risk of short delivery if not squared off.

It is suggested for beginners in stock market not to go for short selling till they are confident and have enough knowledge of stocks and Stock Market.

> *"If money is your hope for independence you will never have it. The only real security that a man will have in this world is a reserve of knowledge, experience, and ability." – Henry Ford*

3.6 Risk Management

Risk Management is the most critical and important factor to manage for working professionals to be successful in stock market.

Whenever we are investing, we have to first think about all the possible risks involved in the investment being made and plan

"The market can stay irrational longer than you can stay solvent."
— John Maynard Keynes

for the mitigation strategy if the investment goes otherwise and not as per expectations.

For any investment we make, the following factors may pose risk to our investment.

- Sudden pulling out of investment by FIIs/DIIs
- Sudden change in Supply and Demand
- Economics and Global Market Scenarios
- Any war like situation anywhere in the world
- Any major change in the policy on Oil and Gas Sector at Domestic or international level
- Any change in the Government or any major change in the Power position in the government
- Any Pandemic like situation which can adversely and drastically affect any particular sector
- Currency fluctuation and Current Event of Things
- Changes in Interest Rate
- Natural calamities
- Investor sentiment and Overall Change in the mood swing of the market
- Stock price manipulation for any particular stock
- Company and related factor like company's own performance may get affected due to various reasons like poor management, rift between major stake

"Accepting losses is the most important single investment device to insure safety of capital." – Gerald M. Loeb

holders, costly raw materials, availability of alternate source or product or substitute in the market and many more.

Managing our investment against so many odds listed above is a real challenge and hence we have to make our strategy in such way that our investment remains safe to a great extent and also its gives a good return. When we invest in equities the major risk is the drastic fall in the price of the stocks to due to any or many factors mentioned above and we have to manage and mitigate such risks which will erode our devalue of investment.

Following strategy will help to manage all the above risks:

Risk Mitigation by Investment Diversification in Different sectors

Businesses are susceptible to several uncertainties that adversely affect their stock prices. To protect the portfolio from big losses, we have to invest in multiple sectors. This ensures that even if some of the sectors do not perform as expected, the other sector minimize their effect on the overall portfolio for the high returns on some of them. We can plan to invest more in the sectors that we are more optimistic about higher returns and less in the other sectors. Diversification also helps to generate the return on regular basis. If we see the historical data, we will find the technology sector, Pharmaceutical sector, Automobile sector, Metal and natural

"If you don't respect risk, eventually they'll carry you out." – Larry Hite

resources sectors have given higher returns as compared to other sectors like, paper, food and beverages, rubber, real estate and others. It makes sense to invest in those sectors which are generally high performing sectors. Also we should keep looking for emerging market and new trends that may come in due to technological advancement or need based demand in the market.

Risk Mitigation by Investment Diversification within Sectors

Sometimes some of sectors performs well but few stock in that sectors may not perform well for many reasons. So it is suggested to diversify within sectors also to an extent so that we get returns from the performing assets within a sector. It is imperative to find the best performing stocks of the different sectors and plan to invest in such stocks. To get regular return from the market, it is suggested to identify few key performers and reap the return on investment on regular basis. Over diversification is also to be avoided which can make us to miss the opportunity of high returns on performing stocks. Generally we can easily find few stocks within a performing sectors which gives good returns and investment in such stocks has to be targeted. Volatility of stocks is another factor where we can keep a close monitoring and plan to invest to get good short term return on regular basis. An investment strategy focused on portfolio creation with mix of high volatility

"Predicting rain doesn't count, building the ark does." – Warren Buffett

growth stocks and value stocks with relatively lesser volatility gives a very good regular return from the market.

Risk Mitigation by Position Sizing and Low initial investment

Low initial investment is key to success as it saves us almost all the risks involved. It has its downside also in case of sudden rise of the stock as in such a scenario we will miss the opportunity of making good profit, but it can also be taken care by keeping close watch on the raising stocks and increasing investment promptly in such stocks. Saving our investment from capital erosion is always recommended than to risk the investment for making high returns. If we remain invested in the market, we are bound to make profit.

Through position sizing rule we never put more than a fixed percent (say – 1% to 4%) of our planned capital into a single trade. So if we have 1,00,000 in our trading account, and we go by 1% rule, then our position in any given asset shouldn't be more than 1000. This risk management strategy also helps us to provide room to find out other trading opportunities as the investment per stock is less and many good stocks can be explored and chosen for investment.

Through fixed amount position sizing rule, we invest a fixed amount per asset and adopt the diversification while building

"Every once in a while, the market does something so stupid it takes your breath away." – By Jim Cramer

the portfolio. This strategy also helps to reduce the risk to a great extent and is easy to implement. The fixed amount has to be so decided that, averaging out the cost at a later date is possible and also the increment on the investment can be done in case the value of investment has to be increased on the asset for higher appreciation in the stock.

Risk Mitigation by Portfolio building on Volatility of Stocks

This is relatively more complex approach on risk management but allows for more flexibility in position sizing based on the volatility of the stock we plan to buy. This approach doesn't allow the same approach on each stock. This approach allows us to exercise finer control over the portfolio. For example if we accumulate more growth stock which are invariably more volatile, then volatility will be reflected in the portfolio. To reduce the overall risk in our portfolio we can buy less of higher volatile stocks and we can expect to see few of the stocks taking the dip and falling sharply and few giving good returns in just few weeks. If we have to take higher risk for higher returns we can plan to build a portfolio with high volatility stocks and less of value stocks. If we are planning for long term investment and returns, we can build portfolio with more value stock and less with growth stock of high volatility.

"Bottoms in the investment world don't end with four-year lows, they end with 10 or 15-year lows." – Jim Rogers

Risk Mitigation by Increasing Investment over a period of time

Increase of investment over a period of time saves us from incorrect timing of the market and we are able to build our portfolio which has stocks purchased at different point of time and hence any sudden change in the market will be taken care automatically. Also this helps us to get returns from the market regularly. This strategy works well for the new investors where they plan to make the investment gradually in the market rather than full investment in one go. This helps to make necessary correction in the investment strategy once we go slow on our investment. This strategy also helps in cost averaging and reducing the risk. High fluctuation and volatility of the market can also be taken care by incremental investment. This strategy is recommended for all new investors and working professionals.

Risk Mitigation for sudden market crash

No one knows when the market will crash and it gives very little time to react to such developments of the market. With the constant bombardment of social media and 24X7 news channel, every piece of small data from the job loss to pandemic, we might think that even taking a break for a cup

"I have been within the four walls of school and I have been on the street. I can confidently tell you that the street is tougher, challenging, daring, exciting and more rewarding. In school; you play alone. But on the street, you play with the big boys." – Ajaero Tony Martins

of coffee could potentially crash the market. Hence we have to remain mentally prepared for such scenarios and be ready with risk mitigation plan. Sudden market crash actually gives more opportunity to get higher return on the investment as the opportunity of market rise has to be enchased with right investment strategy.

Matured investors see this as great opportunity for investment and they find it the best time to make investment to get high and quick returns.

To mitigate such risk, we have to make provision for more investment in such scenarios with help of contingency fund. We can plan and target some of the stocks to get back to profitability based in their market condition and technical chart position and accordingly more investment can be done in such stocks. With this strategy, we can gradually get back most of the stocks to profitability over a period of time and market crash can be converted to an opportunity to make good return from the stock market.

Diversification is another strategy which supports us during market crash as not all stocks fall with same range during market crash. Similarly investment in bluechip companies, keeping a backup plan following a winning formula, rupee cost averaging etc helps not only to beat the market crash but also get very high returns from the market by enchasing the opportunity.

"It can be very expensive to try to convince the markets you are right." – Ed Seykota

Mitigating Risk by Setting Target for booking profit regularly

This is one more way to minimize the risk if we keep on booking our profit at a regular interval on the set target. Some of the investors keep on investing and don't book profit, assuming that in the long run, all the stocks will give profit. But this assumption goes wrong many a times eroding the profit and capital invested.

Booking profit at set target also help to rotate money and grab the opportunity to invest in some new merging stocks. It also helps generating regular income from the market and helps in mitigating the risk of stock falling down again for a longer period. The downside of this strategy is unable encash higher returns on some of the stocks which gives surprisingly very good returns in short span of time. Investors who focus on regular returns and on rotating the money invested can opt for this strategy of risk management and investment.

Risk Mitigation by Pairs Trading

This is a good way to mitigate equity risk when we are anticipating a big price move, but are not sure of its direction. An example is when a significant and important regulatory decision or policy is expected to be made, and we know there will be big move on the price. In such cases, we simultaneously buy the stock of one company and short sell

"Your trading needs to boil down to rules, money management, and that is it." – Michael Covel

(i.e. sell first and cover by buying later) the stocks of another company from the same sector with stop loss on both. This ensures that irrespective of which stock rises or falls, we eventually make profit.

Risk Mitigation by investing in Dividend Paying and Blue Chip Stocks

Companies that have a history of consistent dividend payments are usually strong, established companies and investment in stocks of these companies are always considered safe. Adding such stocks to the portfolio can shield us from market volatility and associated risks.

Established blue chip companies, meanwhile, can be more stable. This extends to their stock prices too. So, we can reduce risk by opting for such stocks in our portfolio.

Such investments are safeguards against the stock market crash also to a great extent.

Risk Mitigation by using stop-losses to limit Loss

A stop-loss point is the price at which an investor will sell a stock and take a loss on the investment. Stop Loss protects us from making excessive losses during sharp market movements against our position. A stop-loss order authorizes the broker to automatically sell or buy a stock when it falls or raises to a

"Amateurs go broke taking large losses, professionals go broke taking small profits." – William Eckhardt

specific level. It also checks our habit to sit on a loss-making stock for too long in the hope that it can rebound.

In addition to static stop losses, we can also use trailing stop loss. For a long position, this is essentially a stop loss that follows the price of the asset as it moves up, but stays put if the asset price starts to go the other way. And vice versa for a short position. A trailing stop allows us to lock-in profit as we make it, by protecting us against significant moves against our position.

Risk Mitigation by investment on Non-Cyclical Stocks in the portfolio

The companies that sells essential goods such as FMGC products, or are into essentials services like banking, insurance, healthcare, illness, and others are comparatively insulated from economic cycles and investment in such companies are relatively safe. These business and services cannot stop irrespective of the state of the economy. There may be reduction in the spending on some of the essential goods and services but there cannot be complete stoppage of these products sale and services. These non-cyclical stocks have relatively stable revenues, which translate into stable stock prices. Making such stocks as part of the portfolio helps to reduce the risk to a great extent.

"Being a successful trader also takes courage: the courage to try, the courage to fail, the courage to succeed, and the courage to keep on going when the going gets tough." – Michael Marcus

Hedging

Hedging, is a risk management strategy. The purpose of hedging risk management strategy is to restrict the losses that may arise due to unexpected fluctuations in the investment prices. Thus we can say that it deals with reducing or eliminating the risk of uncertainty in an investment. It works on the principle of offsetting i.e. taking an opposite and equal position in two different investments. In simple terms, it is hedging one investment by investing in some other investment.

When we plan to hedge, they try to ensure ourselves against a negative event. This does not prevent the event from occurring, but it surely reduces its negative impact. Today, individual investors, portfolio managers and large corporations use this hedging technique to minimize the exposure to various types of risks and decrease the negative impact.

Let us understand Hedging by a simple example. When we buy a life insurance policy, we support and secure your family's future in case of death or any serious injury in some accident. Similarly, when we secure our one investment's loss by offsetting it with another investment's profit, it is known as 'Hedging'. So hedging plays an important role and as a protective device in risk management that has more or less the same effect as insurance but fundamentally differs in operation.

There are many ways to accomplish this objective, including the buying or selling of derivative products like futures and

"You don't have to get in or out of a position all at once. Avoid the temptation of wanting to be completely right." – Jack D. Schwager

options. Derivative is a form of financial tool that is reliant upon (or derived from) an asset (often referred to as the 'underlying asset'). Derivatives are most frequently traded in order to hedge (reduce risk) or speculate (increase risk with the aim of making a high financial gain), and their value is set according to the supply and demand for the underlying asset.

Use of Technology to Reduce the Risk

Artificial Intelligence (AI) is going to be game changer for the stock market in near future which will help reduce the risk on one hand and make right investment on the other.

AI combines a human-like perspective on stocks with the discipline and attention span of a machine.

It will help working professional to make investments easily and accurately based on output which will have data science, deep learning, and machine learning as its input. All major challenges of retail investors will be addressed by Artificial Intelligence and hence investment will be made easy and profitable in stock market.

Already AI is being used and is getting explored and enhanced for cash equity trading, but it is yet to come to masses of investment and trading fraternity.

AI can be utilized in different ways to give us the correct strategies and Input on the market and stocks. For example, AI can analyze millions of data points and execute trades at

"I always say you could publish rules in a newspaper and no one would follow them. The key is consistency and discipline." – Richard Dennis

the optimal price. It can help analyze the data to forecast the market with greater accuracy. It can effectively crunch millions upon millions of data points in real time and capture information.

AI can also use speech recognition and natural language processing technology to save traders time searching through media, websites, conversions, financial data etc. Many use it to generate investment ideas, build portfolios, getting recommendation on daily top stocks using pattern recognition technology and a price forecasting engine.

Some companies have developed fully automated end to end AI trading system that has a strategy engine which observes and analyses potential trades; an order engine that creates orders and performs operational actions; and a logical engine that handles active orders and uses machine learning to improve its performance.

AI is also being used to generate relevant information by gathering and processing data from various sources (news articles, social media postings, financial statements) around the world.

In future, AI may connect the trading communities to increase earnings by scanning markets to find the optimal trading opportunities where deals will be done via blockchain based smart contracts. Many more advance tools are in offing which with enhance the investment and trading to a great extent.

"Trade small because that's when you are as bad as you are ever going to be. Learn from your mistakes." – Richard Dennis

Chapter 4: Facts and Myth of Stock Market

4.1 Misconceptions of the Stock Market

Share Market is for Rich and Needs Investment in Huge Amount.

Share Market provides opportunity from a very small investor to big ones like DIIs and FIIs. Investment in Share market cane be started with a very small amount say Rs. 100 to several thousand crore. We can plan to buy even a single share of company and

"Stock Market bubbles don't grow out of thin air. They have a solid basis in reality, but reality as distorted by a misconception." – George Soros

sell it. Also there are many small investors who regularly get good returns from the market on their investments.

Stock Market provides equal opportunity to all. But the investors and traders have to be disciplined and they should know to pick the right stock for investing and trading and right time to buy and sell.

We must be Intelligent and a Financial Wizard to Start Investing

In fact most of the people who are successful in Stock Market do not have finance background. To be successful in Stock Market, one has to be disciplined and must do required homework before investing and trading. This homework is basically done on analyzing the Fundamental and Technical of the Stock before investing. People who diligently do this, are mostly successful in the stock market. People who speculate and decide their investment and trading based on it are risking their capital in the market and are mostly losers.

Market Forecasts are Reliable

As mentioned in this book on various places, working professionals, due to paucity of time, make their investment decision based on some tips or input received from someone close. They hardly find time to do research and make investment based on the outcome of study and research done about the

"When everything seems to be going against you, remember that the airplane takes off against the wind, not with it." – Henry Ford

stock. So they have to rely on the tips and input received from others which is basically a forecast about the market or stock. Investment done on the information on market forecast never brings the desired result as there are umpteen number of sources who send these forecasts and most of them have different view on the same stock and market.

Hence it is not suggested and recommended to make any investment based on the forecast unless and until it is backed by some study and analysis.

Prices will go up Eventually

If we look at the journey of Sensex we will find that there is significant rise of Sensex since last 20 years. Going by this logic, almost all stocks should have given good return during this period. But it is not so. There are many stocks which have remained stagnant and have not given good return when compared to Sensex. There are some stocks which have sunk during the same period.

During Corona Pandemic in Feb - Mar 2020, there was a steep fall in the Sensex but later the market picked up and crossed the Mar 2020 level. This resulted in many stocks going up exponentially resulting in proving good returns to the investors.

Following are some of the stock which did not pick (Till Feb 2021) up to the level it was in Feb - Mar 2020 and were

"No Price is too low for bear and too high for Bull." – Known

languishing stocks for many who remained invested with these stock shares.

- McLeod Russel India Ltd
- Coal India
- Zee Entertainment Enterprises Ltd
- DB Corp Ltd.
- Jagran Prakashan Ltd
- Indiabulls Housing Finance
- Chalet Hotels Ltd
- EIH Ltd
- Axiscades Technologies Ltd

Stock Market is a good way to make Quick Money

Understanding the Stock Market itself takes lot of time and hence making quick money from the market will remain challenge for most. There are exceptions in all the fields and so in the stock market too.

In general, Stock Market gives good return to them who remain invested and continue in the market for long.

There are other products in the market where people get quick return like future and options. But the risk involved are too high and many small losses eat away the big profit. For many, they book small profits and one big loss nullifies the profit made.

"Rule No. 1: Never lose money. Rule No. 2: Never forget rule No.1"
– Warren Buffett

Investing in the Stock Market is like Gambling

This is a common notion among most of the working professionals that investing in Stock Market is like gambling. If you are lucky, right stock will be picked which will give good return, else you will lose.

Some believe that the moment they start investing, the stock market or the particular day starts going down and they lose. Some believe that the moment they sell their stock, it starts picking up and the prices rise.

There are different misconceptions amongst people which I have come across and their belief is so strong that they quit stock market after taking few chances and never return back for another try.

Fact is that successful investor and traders get good return from the market on regular basis, they get stronger and stronger on their market understanding, and the value of their portfolio keeps growing.

Buying a Falling or Fallen Stock Gives a Good Return

There are umpteen cases where the stocks have fallen never to come back and pick up again. Buying a falling stock and averaging them out with a hope that it will give good return once the price recovers never materializes and all the capital invested erodes never to be recovered again.

"Price is what you pay. Value is what you get." – Warren Buffet

In some cases the stock takes considerable time (5 years and more) to pick up and if investment is done in such stock with a hope that it will give result sometime in future actually makes the investment getting blocked for a very long time which, pragmatically, is not a right investment.

Following are some of the cases where the prices of stock has fallen significantly in past 5 years and have not recovered and have remained stable at the bottom. Investment done in such stocks blocks the capital for circulation.

- Himadri Speciality Chemical Ltd
- Pioneer Distilleries Ltd
- CMI Ltd
- Sumuka Agro Industries Ltd
- Kushal Ltd

"God is such a loving father. He gave every one of us a blank signed check. Anything you write on that check will be yours. But unfortunately; most people die poor because they don't dare to write something big on that check. That check is a gift called life." – Ajaero Tony Martins

4.2 How much Return to expect from Stock Market

Many of us invest in the stock market with the sole purpose of getting rich quickly and fast expecting our investment to grow exponentially. But the fact is that most investors and traders lose money in the market and they stop investing. The main reason for this is that most of us do not accept the fact that it takes time to get the return on the invested money and also there is a certain percentage that market returns if we remain invested. There is data available of the past and the percentage of return for the successful investors and their guidance on

"In the long run, investing is not about markets at all. Investing is about enjoying the returns earned by businesses." – Jack Bogle

return from the market is to taken and accepted to have a realistic view and expectation.

Moreover, many agencies misguide the investors on the percentage of return like stockbrokers, media, fraudsters, etc. These channels claim and promise for high returns in the range of 50 to 200 (even more sometimes) percent annually or half-yearly which don't exist anywhere to the reality.

With all this incorrect information flowing from different directions, a common investor keeps his expectations way too high when they enter the stock market.

What pays off in the stock market is consistency and patience. With consistency and patience, the average return of most of the successful stalwarts has remained in the range of 15 to 25 % annual return. In the bull market and the year when the stock market performs well for most the stocks, the return may even spike to 40% annual return but in the long horizon average return of 15 to 25 % is considered a good return from the market.

Considering all the facts available and the experience, we can conclude that an average return of 15–25% per year can be considered good in the stock market on investments.

We should try to achieve an average return of 15 % per year and then gradually try to increase it.

Trading may give higher returns if planned and executed well.

> *"Value stocks are about as exciting as watching grass grow, but have you ever noticed just how much your grass grows in a week?"*
> *– Christopher Browne*

4.3 Performance of BSE Sensex over the years

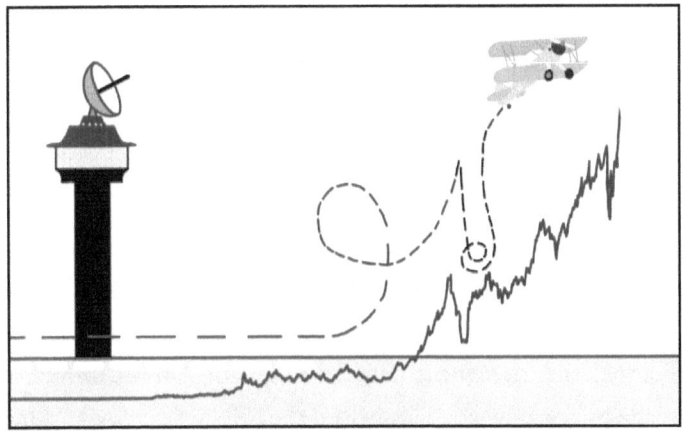

Now, let us walk through the journey of BSE Sensex and let us try to understand the major events in last 40 years.

Pl refer the Sensex graph below.

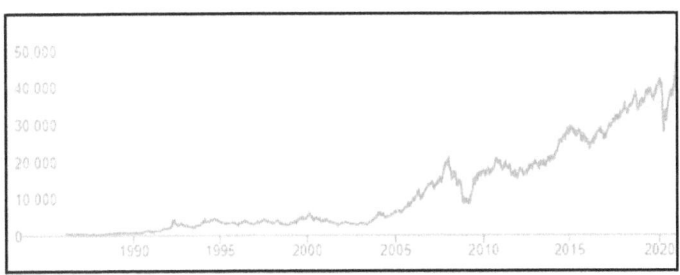

"If You Want to be a Ledge... Find Your Edge..." – Tom Dante

The base value of the SENSEX was taken as 100 on 1 April 1979. The BSE started publishing values of the Sensex in 1985, by then it had moved to the 400-mark. Sensex crossed the 1,000 mark on 25th Jul 1990, 11 years after its launch, on the back of good monsoon and some encouraging corporate results. In this period, the Sensex grew at a CAGR of approx. 23 %.

It took almost a decade to reach 5000 mark on 11th Oct 1999. Crossing 6000 mark was relatively fast as it was achieved on 11th Feb 2000 during the IT Boom period and it remained as record for 4 years until 2nd Jan 2004, when the Sensex closed at 6026.59.

Crossing 7000 mark took considerable time and on 20 June 2005, the news of the settlement between the Ambani brothers boosted the investment and the scripts of Ambani brothers made huge gains too. This helped the SENSEX crossed 7,000 points for the first time. The SENSEX finally closed above the 10,000 mark on 7 February 2006.

Movement of BSE Sensex from 7000 to 12000 was fast paced and every next 1000 points from 7000 took just 1 month to max 3 months' time only mainly due to high investment from FIIs and DIIs.

On 29 October 2007, Sensex crossed the 20,000 mark for the first time during intra-day trading, but closed at lower at 19,977.67 points. However, it was on 11 December

"By living the philosophy that my winners are always in front of me, it is not so painful to take a loss." – Marty Schwartz

Facts and Myth of Stock Market

2007 that it finally closed at a figure above 20,000 points on the back of aggressive buying. While the first 10,000 had taken 27 years, the next 10,000 points came in just 18 months.

Soon SENSEX crossed the 21,000 mark on 8th Jan 2008 for the first time soon, before closing at 20,873. However, it was not until 5 November 2010 that the SENSEX closed at 21,004.96, for its first close above 21,000 points.

Crossing 20000 mark took considerable time. On 10th March 2014 crossed the 22,000 mark for the first time during intraday trading and on 24 March 2014 the index finally closed at 22,095.30.

Milestone 23000 to 28000 was reached in the year 2014 only and hence year 2014 could be considered a good year for the Sensex. Milestone 29000 was reached on 23rd Jan 2015.

Milestone 30,000 was reached on 26th April 2017. Year 2017 saw the next 4 milestones of 31K 32K, 33K and 34K achieved.

Year 2018 saw 4 milestones of 35K, 36K, 37K and 38K achieved and similarly year 2019 saw 3 milestones of 39K, 40K, 41K achieved.

Year 2020 saw all time high achieved with the milestones from 42 K onwards till 49K.

On 21st Jan 2021, Sensex crossed all time High of 50,000 points.

"Sometimes the best trade is no trade." – Anonymous

Major Events on BSE Sensex

- 1990 – Sensex Crosses 1000 points.
- 1991– Manmohan Singh announce liberal budget opening up Indian Economy (1991)
- 1992 – Harshad Mehta Scam
- 1993 – Blast in Mumbai and BSE Building
- 1999 – Kargil War
- 2000 – Technology Boom, Sensex touches 6000
- 2001 – Ketan Parekh Scam, Gujarat Earthquake, attack on Indian Parliament
- 2006 – Sensex Crosses 10000 points
- 2007 – Sensex Crosses 20000 points
- 2008 – Global financial Crisis, leading to Global Market Crash – 2008–2009
- 2009 – Satyam Scam
- 2016 – Demonetization
- 2017 – GST Implemented
- 2020 – Covid Crisis
- 2021 – Sensex Crosses 50000 mark

"One day does not make a trend." – Anonymous

4.4 The Equity/Investment Advisor

Equity Advisors or coach guides us on every step to make the right decision and above all, ensures to help us avoid all the common mistakes that are the cause of big losses for most investors who enter markets to start investing and try their luck. He helps us to develop the right approach, strategy, and realistic expectations about the different investment options.

The stock market is a unique place, which has a huge potential for long-term wealth creation and if we manage to get on a few multi-baggers in our kitty we can make huge profit

"If I'd only followed CNBC's advice, I'd have a million dollars today. Provided I'd started with a hundred million dollars." – Jon Stewart

and wealth over a period of time. Even if we talk about the average long-term returns, return from stock market beats every other asset class by a good margin. Unfortunately, most (around 90% to 95 %) people still manage to lose money in the stock market as they do not have right strategy in place for investment in stock market.

People lose money in the stock market because they go for speculation rather than investment. In Speculation, people purchase a stock or an asset thinking it will become more valuable in the near future. It is a risky financial transaction in the hope to make a profit from short-term fluctuations in the market, rather than attempting to make a profit from the underlying financial attributes embodied in the instrument such as asset strength and value addition, return on investment, or dividends, etc.

Speculative investors tend to make decisions more on the hope or notion about the asset rather than on fundamental analysis of an asset or security.

When we start investing, we are influenced by short-term events to affect our decisions. We become fearful due to short-term volatility. We pick wrong stocks that lead to large portfolio-level losses and eventually we start avoiding stock market and get out of it.

New investors will make mistakes that can be easily avoided by getting the right guidance and involving the right advisor.

"Financial leverage is the advantage the rich have over the poor and middle class." – Rich Dad

Most people invest their money in stocks based on tips received from friends, relatives, and 'well-wishers' who end up losing money, as the people who give the tips do not have enough knowledge for guiding on investment in the stock market. Then there are many other challenges which are explained in the section "Working Professionals: Challenges in the Stock Market.

All of these challenges can be addressed by Equity/Investment Advisors.

A Good Equity/Investment Advisor will help on

- ✓ Research and Analysis
- ✓ Portfolio Building Strategy
- ✓ Buying of Shares
- ✓ Regular Monitoring
- ✓ Buy/Sell/Hold Decisions
- ✓ Wealth Creation

Role of Investment Advisor

A Equity/Investment advisor plays a major to guide

When to buy

When to Sell

How much to invest based on available fund

Which Sector to invest in

What scheme to be adopted for a different stock like short/long terms etc

"The way to get started is to quit talking and begin doing." – Walt Disney

What overall strategy to be adopted for investment based on available fund and the customer's expectations?

What to do with loss-making stocks

To Keep the concerned informed about changes in the polices by Govt

To keep informed about the domestic market scenario and world market

Keep track of underperformers and take the appropriate step needed

Help with the right strategy in case the market crashes

Keep track of value and growth stocks and information about investing in them

Keep track of high dividend-paying companies and inform accordingly

Guide us on fear and greed moment we come across during investing

A good advisor will never give unrealistic promises but will always give a realistic picture and will set the expectations right at the beginning itself. He will help us avoid the common pitfalls that are the cause of big losses for most investors.

In India, people don't recognize the importance of having a coach and guide for their investments. Just by paying a few thousands as fees to their advisors, they can avoid losses worth lakhs due to their wrong investment decisions. Having a good advisor can work wonders for our wealth.

In trading, everything works sometimes and nothing works always."

Summary

At the end of the book "Cruising through the Stock Market", I believe that readers would have understood how to sail through the stock Market volatility and uncertainties to remain invested and get good return on the capital invested with investment of minimum available time with the working professionals.

Stock Market is huge market place for investment with plethora of choices which make it more confusing for investment. Over and above it, the world economy, country's economy, fear of war, oil prices, fear of pandemic, company's performance, sector performance and many other factors decide the share price, its trend and return on investment. Significance of these on the investment is explained in detail and hope the readers would have enjoyed reading it.

The investment and the risk management strategies explained works well for working professionals. To start and get entry in the stock market, the basics of stock market, need to generate additional source of income, major challenges of working professionals with respect to investment in the stock market are explained in detail. The book also provides the practical aspects of investing like, key to success, expected return from the market, different sectors and their past performance, technical analysis and others.

Summary

Readers would also have understood on how to build the portfolio so that associated risk of stock market is taken care and the other required aspects like, disciplined way of investment, goal settings, and winning strategies for working professionals.

In stock market, majority of people lose their money for the different misconceptions about the stock market and common mistakes investors make during investment. These topics are well covered in the book and hope this will add value for the investors.

This book can be a good guide to all who want to start investment in the stock market by learning the basics of stock market and key elements of investment.

www.ingramcontent.com/pod-product-compliance
Lightning Source LLC
Chambersburg PA
CBHW020730180526
45163CB00001B/178